America's Battle for God

America's Battle for God

A European Christian Looks at Civil Religion

Geiko Müller-Fahrenholz

William B. Eerdmans Publishing Company
Grand Rapids, Michigan / Cambridge, U.K.

Published 2007 by
Wm. B. Eerdmans Publishing Co.
2140 Oak Industrial Drive N.E., Grand Rapids, Michigan 49505 /
P.O. Box 163, Cambridge CB3 9PU U.K.

Printed in the United States of America

11 10 09 08 07   7 6 5 4 3 2 1

Library of Congress Cataloging-in-Publication Data

Müller-Fahrenholz, Geiko.
America's battle for God: a European Christian looks at civil religion /
Geiko Müller-Fahrenholz.
p.   cm.
ISBN 978-0-8028-4418-7 (cloth: alk. paper)
1. Christianity and politics — United States.   2. United States — Church history.
3. Religion and politics — United States.   I. Title.
BR115.P7M828   2007
277.3′083 — dc22

2006033205

www.eerdmans.com

To Charlotte and William Johnstone,
Karin and Philip Peterson

In gratitude for forty years of friendship

Contents

—⦿—

Foreword

⟨∞⟩

One hundred and seventy years ago, in the 1830s, when the United States was just fifty years old, an astute Frenchman, Alexis de Tocqueville, toured this country and wrote a book about it, *Democracy in America*. It became a classic set of insights into the enduring "American character." Tocqueville admired much about the young nation, but not everything. Americans, he found, are a very patriotic people. In 1775-1783, their immediate ancestors had battled the world's most powerful empire to win their political freedom. They "think highly of this freedom," he observed, "so highly that they resist mightily all foreign criticism of their new nation." Indeed, said Tocqueville, "nothing is more annoying in the ordinary intercourse of life [here] than the irritable patriotism of the Americans. A foreigner will gladly agree to praise much in their country, but he would like to be allowed to criticize something, and that he is absolutely denied."

Tocqueville would have appreciated the distinctions drawn in a sermon by William Sloane Coffin, Jr.:

> There are three kinds of patriots, two bad, one good. The bad are the uncritical lovers and the loveless critics. Good patriots carry on a lover's quarrel with their country, a reflection of God's lover's quarrel with all the world.

Uncritical patriotism often stems from weakness and insecurity, as might be illustrated by Stephen Decatur's famous 1815 toast: "To my country! May she ever be right, but right or wrong, my country!" Would that Decatur had said: "When right, may she remain so; when wrong, may she be set right." Uncritical love of country is an invitation to blithe amorality, just as loveless criticism is an invitation to cynical moralism.

Any Americans who pick up this book will have the maturity of their patriotism severely tested. Christians among us will have the maturity of our faith and its associated ethics tested. Psalm 15:4 defines the "righteous" as those who are willing to "swear to their own hurt." They assent to truth about themselves even if that truth is painful. This book, by its very publication in English by an American press, is meant to be read by us Americans. Will many of us read it? I hope so. Amid the current swirls of politics in my country, however, I'm not so sure. Immediately after 9/11, new bursts of uncritical patriotism erupted across our land from the Atlantic to the Pacific. The president of the United States responded to the event with "amazement" that any foreigner should display "vitriolic hatred" toward America because, he said, "I know how good we are." In those days some Americans asked, briefly, "Why do they hate us?" That question is the title and subject of chapter 4 of this book. For the U.S. president, the question was obviously merely rhetorical. Like him, few of my American neighbors spent much time searching for an answer, which reminded me of a line from Swinburne: "'What is truth?' Pilate asked, but stayed not for an answer."

These pages will furnish any patient American reader with some answers. But reading them may not be a very pleasant experience, any more than reading about the crimes of Nazism was pleasant for generations of Germans after World War II. Even to suggest such a comparison, of course, is to rouse great anger among some potential readers, to whom I feel bound to say the following:

> This book comes from the mind and heart of a German theologian and churchman who knows so much about this country, who has lived in and near our borders so often, and who loves America so much that his criticisms emerge from his grief and

mourning over the threat to the best in American history from the worst.

It comes as well from a German national who loves his country, too, but who in his post-1945 adult life has endured rising domestic confrontation with one of the most undoubtedly evil forms of politics in world history — Nazism. Over several generations, Germans have had to face the challenge of rescuing some continuing pride in their history while experiencing a deep shame for parts of that history.

Combining pride and shame is a hard struggle for us humans. This author has been deeply engaged in that struggle in Germany. As he says in chapter 2, "The burden of sorrow and fear that we Europeans carry is that we have lived the history of hating enemies and destroying them so many times."

Finally, this book comes from a Christian theologian who counts on the reality of ecumenical fellowship to transcend the barriers of world nationalisms and to open the ears of Christians in this country to the possible wisdom and worldviews of our partners-in-faith in other countries. To read these pages patiently will require of an American Christian a decisive, conscious theological distinction between the loyalty we owe the United States of America and the loyalty we owe the God and Father of Jesus Christ our Lord. The failure of some Christians among us to make that distinction clearly — symbolized by American flags in numerous churches across the land — is one of the contemporary tragedies of religious life in America. Geiko Müller-Fahrenholz grieves over this tragedy. So do I.

I am not alone among Americans in sharing this grief. This book leaves me with a worry not only about the current splits between my nation and other nations, but also about the *internal* splits between different groups of citizens and between groups of religious people in America over our country's current roles in the world. I picture some of us picking this book up and throwing it down angrily, and others of us reading to the end with tears in our eyes. There is anger in this book, but I hope no reader will neglect to feel the well of sorrow from which even the anger flows.

Müller-Fahrenholz is conscious of some enormous good that our country has done in the world in his lifetime, not the least being our costly success in rescuing Europe from totalitarianism and from the threats of economic disaster in the 1940s and '50s. Like many thoughtful Germans, he is aware of our acclaimed democratic virtues. He believes that they have been worth imitating in other nations over the past two centuries. But he is also aware that no nation has a monopoly on either political or moral virtue, and that a super-assurance of the virtue of one's own nation flies in the face of fact and also in the face of a Christian view of our humanity. Reinhold Niebuhr used to say, "There is only one empirically verifiable claim in the Christian faith: 'All have sinned and fall short of the glory of God.'" Curiously enough, many voices from the so-called evangelical right agree with this verse from Paul (Romans 3:23) as it applies to us sinners as individuals, but not to us as a political body known as the United States of America. Unfortunately, many of the most honored leaders in American history have fed this contradiction: for example, Thomas Jefferson called America an "innocent nation in a wicked world"; John Adams said that some day our country will "govern the world and introduce the perfection of man." Such views led to the "American exceptionalism" that Tocqueville encountered — the reckless belief that Americans are God's chosen instrument for saving the world.

Faithful reading of the Bible and diligent study of the great theologians should have spared the Christians of this nation any such illusions. In all realism, most of the rest of humanity will not accept the right of Americans to define justice, democracy, correct belief, and righteous living for all the peoples of earth. Nor will the wise among them accept the claim that any nation, including America, is virtuous in every influence it exerts on others. As Müller-Fahrenholz comments in chapter 5, "The [9/11] attacks hit individually innocent people, but they did not hit a nation innocent in its use of power." In all periods of history, claims to political innocence are easily refuted by people who suffer from governments whose agents, however well intentioned, always do some evil while doing some good. The daily news illustrates this perpetually when it is honest news: governments are fallible servants of justice.

This German Christian comes close to the central message of his book when he struggles over these matters out of some deep roots in his theology:

> [T]here needs to be a way of connecting greatness and guilt, progress and failure. . . . This appears to be impossible. But my response as a Christian would be this: it is not only possible, it is in fact inevitable that we live by the grace of God and yet fall from grace. This is the real power of the Christian faith: that the grace of God is great enough to accept the sinfulness of human beings and to offer the chance to change their ways. This is what repentance and conversion are about.

But sometimes human beings and their governments change their ways for the worse. In responding to the welcome invitation to write a foreword for this book, I encountered an anxiety that has never afflicted me in putting words to paper over my career of fifty years as an American theologian. I have had to wonder: Will the U.S. government, in its unprecedented "war against terror," monitor these pages? Will the criticisms of America in this book be subject to some form of government censorship? Will the courage of Eerdmans Publishing Company — and its tax status — become the object of a government investigation before these pages see public light? How embarrassed I am, how ashamed, that such questions should even *occur* to me in free America! Surely the host of fine theological books coming out of Grand Rapids have long since marked this press as worthy of the trust that the First Amendment puts in us citizens when it mandates the free exercise of religion and the press. Surely no government agency will review this foreword after I put it in the mail. . . . Surely?

Let me end with two illustrations, one that reinforces my anxiety expressed above, another that helps to allay it. Both come out of links between Americans and Germans.

In May 2004, a hundred or so members of a Manhattan church gathered to view Martin Doblmeier's recently completed documentary on the life and death of Dietrich Bonhoeffer. Afterwards, led by a panel of scholars, audience discussion focused on the question: Are we

Americans at a Bonhoeffer moment? Are we in a time when nationalism will overtake our churches, and freedom to listen to voices from
the rest of the world will get drowned out by our rush to defend ourselves against foreign enemies? Are we at a time when, like Bonhoeffer,
we must resist the enemies of democracy inside our own nation? The
pros and cons of answers went back and forth for an hour. The time
for closing had come when a tall elderly man stood up to make a final
comment; it ended the meeting and reduced the audience to stunned silence: "I am a survivor of Auschwitz," he said. "I do not think that we
are yet at a Bonhoeffer moment in America. I think that we are at
1932."

In October 2005 I shared this story with several leaders of the
Evangelical Church in Germany, colleagues of the author of this book.
I shared my anxieties about the fragility of democracy and freedom in
the current affairs of my own country. I told them that I shared many
of their criticisms of American roles in current world affairs. But toward the end of the conversation, they turned to me and said: "We
have confidence that the United States has a way of correcting itself.
Your country taught ours how, in a democracy, we can correct ourselves. We believe that your country still has that capacity."

May that be so. And may this book help it to be so.

DONALD W. SHRIVER, JR.
President Emeritus,
Union Theological Seminary,
New York

Introduction

—◦◦◦—

This book is a foreigner's attempt to understand religious under-
currents in the public culture and political life of the United States
of America, or, to put it a bit more succinctly and emphatically, an outsider's view of America's God. I have written it in the hope that a perspective from abroad may be able to cast in starker relief some parts of
the picture that are otherwise too close for Americans to notice. However, I do understand that some of my observations may well be painful for Americans to read — even if they might tend to agree with
them. It is never comfortable to have one's own country criticized by
strangers.

So why do I try it? And what are my qualifications for doing so? It
may be helpful for me to start by telling the story of my encounters
with America.

A Year at Yale

It began forty years ago, in August 1965, when I set foot on American
soil for the first time. I had just finished my theological training at German universities and was searching for a university where I could do

graduate work on ethical problems. I did not have a moment of doubt that these interests would compel me to travel to America. So I applied to the World Council of Churches in Geneva for a scholarship. And, to my great surprise, I was sent to Yale University Divinity School in New Haven, Connecticut.

To this day I do not know who was responsible for placing me at Yale Divinity. In my application I had indicated an interest in some lesser-known seminaries because I assumed that Yale was something for the chosen few, among whom I, a farmer's son, certainly did not belong. And yet there I was — and I loved it. To be sure, the Divinity School made me work hard, but it was gratifying work because of Yale's fantastic opportunities for study.

Thus I came to know America at its best — at least in some ways. Yale combined great scholarship with political and social commitment. It stood for the values that had established the claim of the United States to be the leading power among Western democracies. I remember the fervent discussions that took place in the "common room" regarding the civil rights movement launched by Martin Luther King, Jr., as well as concerns about America's growing military involvement in Vietnam. Like its Ivy League competitors, Yale claimed a role in the nation's life — in fact, in the life of the world's nations. I got a feeling for that in the graduation ceremony of 1966, when I received my degree as a "Master of Sacred Theology." During that ceremony, honorary doctorates were conferred on leading figures from the realms of culture, science, and politics. This claim was reflected a few years later in a statement by Yale's president: "Anyone who cares about civilization should care about Yale." I considered that a bit of a mouthful at the time; but it did say something about the confident self-understanding of the university and its sense of mission.

There was another side to my year at Yale. Together with some other foreign students, I worked in the Divinity School's kitchen — for $1.25 per hour, if I remember correctly — and I became familiar with the staff people who ran the kitchen. The manager was an Italian woman, and all the others were black women and men. Eventually, they would take us to their churches. A growing sense of trust and friendship enabled them to talk to us about what really mattered to them. And thus I got a glimpse of a world within America that was quite different from the one I saw from the viewpoint of Yale professors and students, one in which people struggled with terrible memories and burning injustices.

The Bitterness of Immigrants

The tight schedule during the academic year at Yale prevented me from traveling around the whole of the United States, as I had wished to do. But I did go as far south as Washington, D.C., as far north as the Niagara Falls, and as far west as St. Louis. That was not much of America; even so, there was one thing that struck me: the sameness of buildings, of restaurants, and of drinks and foods. Kentucky Fried Chicken, for instance, had the same red roof wherever I went. And it was the same with pizza places, and with other restaurants or businesses, even before McDonald's had become such a pervasive presence in the fast-food industry.

I was looking at all this, of course, through my European lenses. Back home, architectural styles, food, and eating and drinking habits would change profoundly within a few hundred miles. So I wondered why Americans would want to have the same kinds of experiences all over their vast country, despite the great variety of landscapes and climates. There was also a toughness and recklessness in America that was both fascinating and worrisome to me. It was not until much later that I observed the considerable differences between, say, Vermont and southern Virginia, between towns in Minnesota and California.

There was another matter that moved me deeply. In St. Louis, I stayed with a friend who had a scholarship at Eden Theological Seminary. Part of his assignment was to look after a small German-speaking congregation some thirty miles west of the Mississippi River.

One Sunday morning, while he prepared for the service, I walked around in the cemetery that surrounded the small church. A gravestone that had a German inscription caught my eye. It gave the name of the dead woman, the date of her birth, and the name of the town in Germany where she was born, Wilhelmshafen, close to the town where I was born. But what really struck me was the final line of the inscription: *Gestorben in der Fremde* ("died in a foreign land").

Here lay the remains of an immigrant who had lived in America for many years, and yet her gravestone revealed that it had remained a foreign land for her. Apparently, she had felt like a foreigner in America for many long years. She remembered her roots back in Wilhelmshafen, but she seemed not to have put down new roots in the Great Plains west of St. Louis. I sensed a pain there that brought tears to my eyes. And I began to see the pain of uprootedness that characterizes the origins of so many millions of American immigrant families. To be sure, most of them were more than happy to leave behind what must have been for them oppressive conditions, political pressures, social inequalities, financial desperation, or religious persecution. And yet, by cutting themselves off from their native lands, they had lost homes, friends, and beloved relatives whom they would very likely never see again. As they struggled with all their might to make a living in this new land, there must have remained a hidden wound from which there was no healing. So it just had to be "forgotten." But did this pain, unacknowledged though it must have been in most cases, explain Americans' widespread disregard for the past? Was this the dark shadow that accompanied America's pragmatism and its citizens' preoccupation with the future?

The Encounter with American Protestantism

Ten years later, from 1974 to 1979, I worked with the World Council of Churches. This position involved several extended trips to various locations in the United States, and I became acquainted with many American theologians and people who had leadership responsibilities within the church. At the time it appeared that many concerns voiced from around the world were having a strong impact on American churches; and U.S. churches were playing a stronger role in the life of the churches worldwide as well.

And yet those of us who were committed to the ecumenical movement in those years were not fully aware that large sectors of American Protestantism were out of our reach. Although we believed that we were addressing central concerns in the lives of the churches, we were considered to be "to the left" by those who were silently holding on to what they considered the "fundamentals" of the Christian faith. So it came as a surprise to us that, during the presidential campaign of Ronald Reagan, the "Moral Majority" turned out to be a formidable political force. Since that time — over the past twenty-five years — the Christian right has become immensely influential, while classical "mainstream" Protestantism appears to be losing influence. The famous 475 Riverside Drive, the New York headquarters of the National Council of Churches in the United States — indeed a center of the worldwide church — is simply not what it used to be.

Whether or not they were active in the ecumenical movement, many observers from outside the United States found it difficult to understand what the powerful right-wing evangelicals stood for. I know of no place in Europe with anyone comparable to the U.S. televangelist, whose influence reaches into the highest echelons of political power. That there should be heated debates between evolutionists and creationists is simply inconceivable. Europe is thoroughly secularized, or, in other words, religiously illiterate. Therefore, most observers in Europe don't know how to relate to the religious language that appears to be quite normal on the other side of the Atlantic. They do not understand the "God-talk" of political leaders in the United States and have no way of assessing its impact on global policies. This is one factor among others that accounts for the growing estrangement between the United States and Europe.

For me, a new kind of America began to emerge, and I saw it partly as a shift in the role that religion was allowed to play in politics. This book is an attempt to understand what is at stake here.

The Haunting Presence of the Vanished People

During those extended travels across the United States, I began to realize how many of the names of cities and states, of rivers and mountains, were taken from the missing peoples who had once lived there:

Connecticut, Massachusetts, Chicago, Manhattan, Susquehenna, Chesapeake, Mississippi, Milwaukee, Oklahoma. These and many more names had a haunting quality for me because they spoke of those native people who were betrayed, expelled, and murdered — mostly by immigrants from Europe, among whom were many of my fellow Germans. Yet most Americans I encountered seemed to be unaware of the silent cry that these names carry with them. They appeared to be unaware of the genocidal part of their history. What did it cost, I wondered, to "forget" the silent message of so many names? What did this say about the reality and power of denial?

Obviously, I was attuned to such questions because, as a member of Germany's post–World War II generation, I grew up with tormenting discussions about the "how" and the "why" of the near-genocide of the Jewish people in Europe by the Third Reich. I realize, of course, that my American counterparts would be appalled if I compared the Holocaust of the Jewish people to the exterminating warfare directed at the Native American peoples. I am not suggesting any comparisons — for the simple reason that crimes of such heinous proportions defy any comparison. Rather, my point is to investigate how peoples and nations remember (and easily forget) those parts of their past that are cruel and laden with guilt. This, too, is a concern that began to influence my reflections about America, and it will play a part in this book.

Living in America's Back Yard

From 1988 to 1993, I taught at two universities in Costa Rica. Life in this small Central American country confronted me with a distinctly different way of looking at the United States. I lived among people who also thought of themselves as "Americans," in the sense of belonging to the continent of America. This implied that they believed that the citizens of the *Estados Unidos* had no right to speak of themselves as "Americans" as if they were the only ones on this continent who mattered. But, of course, the issue was not about terminology. At stake was a much deeper and more painful issue that became apparent in the economic, political, and cultural relationships between the small

Latino countries and the overwhelmingly powerful neighbor to the north. To be sure, they were fascinated by the way of life of the "gringos," so much so that Miami could well be called the co-capital of Central America and the Caribbean. But even their fascination seemed to aggravate the anger with which most of my colleagues and students looked at the superpower to the north.

Was it envy that caused this anger? I don't think so. I believe it was, rather, the experience of being seen as second-rate human beings. Or, to put it differently, it was the everyday experience of the glaring discrepancies between the democratic liberties propounded in Washington, D.C., on the one hand, and the apparent imperialism of the same U.S. government that was reflected in the support of oppressive régimes in Central America and elsewhere, on the other hand. The Monroe Doctrine (1823), developed during the first decades of the nineteenth century, was for Central Americans the beginning of a "matrix of control" by which every country south of the Rio Grande was dominated to some degree by the United States. Mexico, Nicaragua, Panama, and Cuba had special stories to tell; but even the long civil wars in El Salvador and Guatemala could not be understood without the heavy military and financial support of U.S. forces. I sensed the weight of these painful memories wherever I went. Why? Because experiences of impotence and humiliation keep burning in the hearts of people. "We live in the back yard of the U.S." was a common statement. In other words, they felt themselves at the mercy of a very big brother to the north, and this has created the love-hate relationship that I encountered everywhere in Central and South America.

Forty Years Later — Reflections in 2006

Where am I now, more than forty years after arriving at Yale? I am just as fascinated by America as I was then. I like to spend time with Americans. The ones I have encountered have been open-minded and generous, polite and humorous, and reliable friends. But, of course, the more I learn about the United States, the less I can confidently know. In his book *Travels with Charley* (1961), John Steinbeck called his native country a "monster" because it was far too big and too diverse for him to grasp. If it was true for him, how much more is it true for an outsider like me!

And yet, "we live on images," as psychologist and historian Robert Jay Lifton once said. The images he refers to are the models and paradigms that guide our lives, something close to what Germans call *Weltanschauung,* that is, the ways we perceive the world. This implies that our humanity depends on our willingness to work on these images, to share them with others, and to have them challenged by others. Obviously, "America" is an essential part of the images by which I live. This applies not only to me as an individual, and not only to the church of which I am a member, but also to my people. As a matter of fact, what happens in the United States is of global concern: what the world's only superpower does or decides not to do affects us all. This is why I think that outsiders like me have good reasons to offer our views of developments in the United States. Limited though my views may be, they may be able to contribute to a much-needed debate about our common future.

I CANNOT CLOSE these opening remarks without expressing my sincere gratitude to John Shelton Lawrence. Not only am I indebted to him for his scholarly work, but he has also dedicated many hours of his time to work on my English, to check references, and to offer critical corrections. My thanks also to Donald W. Shriver, Jr., who was kind enough to write the foreword to this book. His penetrating work on the power of reconciliation in the lives of nations has encouraged me and helped me do my work. I am very grateful to William B. Eerdmans Publishing Co. for publishing my book, and to Reinder Van Til for using his editorial skills to improve my text.

As I indicated at the beginning, I know that it is not easy to accept critical remarks, least of all those of a foreigner. Yet it is my hope that, as they read between the lines of this book, readers will discover the love and concern with which I have written it.

GEIKO MÜLLER-FAHRENHOLZ
Bremen, Germany

CHAPTER 1

"God Bless America":
The Messianic Experiment

—◦◦◦—

When a president of the United States closes an address with the words "God bless America," many observers in secularized Europe shake their heads in disbelief. And they shake their heads even more over the fact that a majority of U.S. citizens do not seem to object to this kind of "God-talk." The differences between our cultures are significant. On our side of the Atlantic, we have come to rather different stances regarding the role of religion in politics. An interesting example can be found in the ardent discussions about references to God in the proposed constitution for the European Community. In the end, all such references were rejected. And the fact that France and the Netherlands said no to the proposal for a European constitution had nothing to do with this aspect.

Given their current secular bias, most European politicians and political scientists regard the religious rhetoric of political leaders in the United States as opportunistic attempts to fulfill the expectations of certain religious groups. Even if this were the case — and to some extent it undoubtedly is — one would have to note the fact that "God bless America" as political currency seems to reward anyone who consistently invokes the divine. In other words, the religious component in the United States is influential enough to shape the political language, whereas in Europe no election can be won by playing to the religious feelings of people. It seems clear that, in Europe, such religious groups are too small to require special catering by politicians. Generally speaking, this turning away from public piety reflects a widespread uneasiness about mixing religion with politics.

It took me a while to recognize that the religious rhetoric of leaders in the United States is part and parcel of the nation's political culture. Professor Jürgen Moltmann (my *Doktorvater,* teacher, and friend at Tübingen University) helped me realize that the religious language of President George W. Bush, though much more explicit than that of many of his predecessors, is part of the great tradition that has influenced the development of the United States from its very beginnings.[1] This is the messianic tradition that makes "America" such a loaded term. In its full sense, "America" is a huge country with a great mission, a historical entity endowed with an exceptional promise.

The Messianic Heritage

Moltmann's perspective on "America" as a messianic project led me to take a closer look at its historical development, and that drew me all the way back to the Pilgrim fathers.[2] When they had reached the coast of the "New World," after a fearfully long and dangerous voyage, they were deeply convinced that their undertaking had been guided and protected by God. Between 1619 and 1640, more than 20,000 Puritans arrived, and they thought of themselves as the new Israel. They called the land they had left behind "Pharaoh's Britain," a land of servitude. What they saw ahead of them was the new and uncorrupted land of new beginnings. And just as the Israelites of old had to fight against

1. See, especially, Jürgen Moltmann, *The Coming of God: Christian Eschatology* (Minneapolis: Fortress Press, 1995), pp. 168-78. A *Doktorvater* is a dissertation supervisor.

2. Two books I found particularly informative: Robert N. Bellah, *The Broken Covenant: American Civil Religion in Time of Trial,* 2nd ed. (Chicago/London: University of Chicago Press, 1992), esp. chs. 1 and 2; Richard T. Hughes, *Myths America Lives By* (Urbana/Chicago: University of Illinois Press, 2004).

the Philistines, so the new "Israelites" saw themselves commissioned to do battle with the heathen peoples for the possession of what they regarded as their promised land.

It could not be otherwise. The most important book for the first immigrants — in fact the only book most of them possessed — was the Bible. Holy Scripture provided them with the images that gave their lives meaning. Most impressive among the biblical stories was the account of how God's people had been set free from the bondage of Egypt. It told how the Israelites had left Egypt on their great Exodus; how their leader, Moses, had fought with them over the Ten Commandments and their purity as the people of God; how Joshua had fought many battles to free the Promised Land from the heathen who inhabited it. This grand narrative, together with the fiery words of the ancient prophets and the mighty psalms of David, provided the framework for the lives of these immigrants, for the prospects of their communities, and, at a later stage, for their formation of a union. The "city on the hill"! The "light of the world"! These images formed the vision of America — the Promised Land for the chosen people.

The images portrayed an exciting project that attracted millions of people from Europe, including from my home country. Wherever women and men found the pressures of feudal landlords unbearable, wherever they suffered under the absolutist powers of kings and queens, wherever they could no longer stand the churches that oppressed their beliefs — they sought America as a land to which to escape. As the Statue of Liberty in the harbor of New York City later signaled to those who came across the Atlantic Ocean, it promised to be a haven of freedom — at least for those who came from Europe. For those who came from Africa, of course, it was a gruesomely different affair: for them, "freedom" meant that someone else had the right to own human beings as property.

Here, in the land of the free, everything would be better. No kings would rule; the people themselves would govern. No pope would determine what his subjects had to believe; the fellowship of believers, faithfully listening to Scripture, would become the true church of God. The land was vast. If you could not make it in the East, you could go to the West, where new opportunities lay waiting. The Declaration of

Independence promised the right to the "pursuit of happiness" to everyone who was courageous enough to go for it.

In the course of time the biblical images lost their direct meaning, but their messianic character persisted. America became the land of unlimited possibilities. Limits and borders would not stop the advancing settlers and conquerors; rather, they were regarded as frontiers, that is, as limits to be transcended and mysteries to be explored. And thus "progress" became a term laden with messianic meaning: it carried with it the fascination of the early settlers and their quest for the kingdom of God in the New World. Yet, as a promise, it was rather demanding: you could be the architect of your own fortune, but you had to be ready to grasp it, to hold on to it, and to fight for it. That was — and is — the way you lived up to your calling.

There is a considerable dose of individualism in this image of progress. Recognizing it helps us understand why there is such a multitude of communities and churches, such a proliferation of interest groups and societies. To be sure, there has been a good deal of fragmentation and secularization over the centuries, so much so that the biblical foundations of the earlier generations have become obscure. But much of the old millennialist ethos is still alive and well. The vision of America was linked not only to the Exodus tradition of the Israelites, but equally forcefully to the end-time images of the Bible, especially those found in the book of Revelation. The Second Coming of Christ and the inauguration of his millennial rule would include a final battle with the Antichrist, and this gave special importance to the creation of the United States: it was seen as a part of the "Thousand-Year Kingdom" that was about to come.

As I will show in the next chapter, this millennialism has provoked a plethora of expectations and speculations. The political theology implied in the bestselling *Left Behind* series, for instance, makes clear that millennialist concepts are organic to the idea that America has a God-given calling for the entire world. It does not exist for itself alone but has a redeeming function for the other nations of the earth. Even where the biblical origins are no longer understood, the sense of mission has stayed alive. This is what strikes me as the messianic project, the specific sense of mission for the American nation. It cannot be imagined without the idea of a divine power that guides and sustains the American calling.

Once one gets a feeling of this dynamic, it is easy to understand why the Puritans of the early years favored theocratic concepts. What had been corrupted in England, they would make a reality in the New World. With God as the true sovereign, church and society together were called to lead a God-fearing life. Based on Holy Scripture, there would evolve a "holy, Christian Commonwealth" — in other words, a unique political and social system in which church and state were constituted as a covenantal community with God.[3]

Of course, as more and more immigrants flooded into the new land, and as relations between the New England communities and the ones in the South (e.g., Virginia) became more intimate, that clear theocratic vision grew dim. What remained, however, was the reference to God — or, in the language of the Enlightenment period, to the Supreme Being — as a guiding concept for the self-understanding of the emerging American nation. Perhaps it is even appropriate to conclude that the messianic drive became an independently compelling attraction for all the strangers who flocked to this new country. Consequently, the political leaders would evoke it in order to rally the people behind them and to give the people a sense of belonging. This would also explain why this messianism could be adapted to the perceived needs and aspirations of the United States as its citizenry grew and expanded beyond anything imaginable in the early days. This would also explain why public discourse retained a need for such a strong religious component.

It is revealing to look at the U.S. presidents' inaugural addresses. They constitute singular moments in which an incoming president will strive to connect his program to the messianic project of the nation. The first president of the United States, George Washington, for instance, declared in his first inaugural address:

[I]t would be peculiarly improper to omit in this first official act my fervent supplications to the Almighty Being who rules the

---

3. See Avihu Zakai, *Exile and Kingdom: History and Apocalypse in the Puritan Migration to America* (New York: Cambridge University Press, 1992), p. 11.

universe, who presides in the councils of nations and whose providential aids can supply every human defect, that his benediction may consecrate to the liberties and happiness of the people of the United States a Government instituted by themselves for these essential purposes, and may enable every instrument employed in its administration to execute the functions allotted to its charge.

Washington goes on in this vein to describe the historic task of this young federation of states:

No people can be bound to acknowledge and adore the Invisible Hand which conducts the affairs of men more than those of the United States. Every step by which they have advanced to the character of an independent nation seems to have been distinguished by some token of providential agency.

He later adds:

[S]ince we ought to be no less persuaded that the propitious smiles of Heaven can never be expected on a nation that disregards the eternal rules of order and right which Heaven itself has ordained; and since the preservation of the sacred fire of liberty and the destiny of the republican model of government are justly considered, perhaps, as deeply, as finally, staked on the experiment entrusted to the hands of the American people. . . .[4]

These statements seem to show that:

(1) The God of whom George Washington speaks is the almighty Lord of the universe who guides the "councils of nations," while his "invisible hand" governs the new nation's history.

4. "First Inaugural Address of George Washington, April 30, 1789" (Avalon Project of Yale Law School: http://www.yale.edu/lawweb/avalon/presiden/inaug/wash1.htm [accessed Nov. 5, 2005]).l

(2) God's providence guides the "experiment" entrusted to the American people. The struggle for independence is thus seen as a goal of providence itself.

(3) This struggle is about the "holy fire of freedom." Linked with the republican model of government, it is meant to be "deeply . . . finally, staked on the experiment entrusted to the hands of the American people." In this way, liberty and the republican model of government constitute the center of the "experiment" to which the United States is forever committed.

It is understandable that George Washington should have interpreted the unequal struggle between the small American settler-planter colonies against the overwhelmingly powerful England as a liberating action of the Almighty. In connecting the American experiment to the purposes and powers of heaven, he struck a tone that echoes through the war messages and inaugural addresses of many of his successors. Here are some examples from twentieth-century presidents. Woodrow Wilson's statement of his war aims in 1917 is particularly eloquent: "The world must be made safe for democracy. Its peace must be planted upon the tested foundations of political liberty. We have no selfish ends to serve. We desire no conquest, no dominion. We seek no indemnities for ourselves, no material compensation for the sacrifices we shall freely make. We are but one of the champions of the rights of mankind."[5]

Franklin D. Roosevelt also carried the mantle of world redemption comfortably when, in his fourth inaugural address (in 1945), he said: "The Almighty God has blessed our land in many ways. He has given our people stout hearts and strong arms with which to strike mighty blows for freedom and truth. He has given to our country a faith which has become the hope of all peoples in an anguished world. So we pray to Him now for the vision to see our way clearly — to see the way that leads to a better life for ourselves and for all our fellow men — to the achievement of His will to peace on earth."[6]

5. Woodrow Wilson, "President Woodrow Wilson's War Message, April 2, 1917," *War Messages*, 65th Cong., 1st Sess., Senate Doc. No. 5, Serial No. 7264, Washington, D.C., 1917, pp. 3-8, *passim*.

6. Franklin D. Roosevelt, "Fourth Inaugural Address, January 20, 1945" (Avalon

John F. Kennedy concluded his inaugural address with these words: "With a good conscience as our only sure reward, with history the final judge of our deeds, let us go forth to lead the land we love, asking His blessing and His help, but knowing that here on earth God's work must truly be our own."[7] These statements forcefully convey the image of messianic destiny as the backbone of the "national religion"; or, expressed another way, the political aims of the United States are seen from within as divinely inspired and therefore endowed with an element of messianic inerrancy. It is within this lineage that President George W. Bush said in his State of the Union Address of January 28, 2003:

> America is a strong nation, and honorable in its use of our strength. We exercise power without conquest, and we sacrifice for the liberty of strangers. Americans are a free people, who know that freedom is the right of every person and the future of every nation. The liberty we prize is not America's gift to the world, it is God's gift to humanity.[8]

These words contain three convictions that may help outsiders understand the peculiar strands of American messianism:

(1) Freedom is God's gift to humanity.
(2) America has embodied this "gift" so fully that other nations could mistake it for "America's gift" to the world. The fact that America has appropriated God's gift of freedom implies America's special mandate to bring liberty to all other nations.
(3) America "sacrifices" herself for the freedom of strangers. Hence it

---

Project at Yale Law School: http://www.yale.edu/lawweb/avalon/presiden/inaug/fr0054 .htm [accessed Nov. 20, 2005]).

7. "The Inaugural Address of John F. Kennedy, January 20, 1961" (Avalon Project at Yale Law School: http://www.yale.edu/lawweb/avalon/presiden/inaug/kennedy.htm [accessed Nov. 5, 2005]).

8. George W. Bush, "President Delivers State of the Union" (White House release: http://www.whitehouse.gov/news/releases/2003/01/20030128-19.html [accessed Oct. 30, 2005]).

is an act of sacrificial commitment for America to bring the divine gift of liberty to strangers in other lands.

The element of sacrifice adds special meaning to the messianic project.

If all of this is true, the United States emerges in the exceptional position that Ernest Lee Tuveson has labeled the "redeemer nation."[9] Such a claim sounds terribly arrogant. But before one denounces this as a self-deceiving justification for any use or misuse of power, I wish to quickly acknowledge that it has often been substantiated by a generous and costly commitment that many men and women — not least in my country, Germany — will never forget. Not only can the interventions of the United States in World War I and World War II be characterized in just such terms; the rapid re-establishment of democratic rule after Hitler's "Thousand Years' Reich" must be attributed largely to the costly involvement of the American people. Furthermore, I wish the reader to keep in mind that other nations have made such messianic claims. Again, as a German, I cannot but be mindful of Hitler's political messianism. He claimed to be called by "Providence" to rid the world of the contaminating evil of the Jewish people. Jürgen Moltmann has called this "the terrible but short-lived German caricature of this idea."[10]

What makes the messianism of the United States unique — and threatening — is the fact that it is an active element of its "historical script." It appears to justify the American sense of global power and commitment. Thus the question arises: How can a nation sustain a messianic self-image without falling into the trap of arrogant nationalism? Is the messianic project of America forever immune to any misuse? For instance, is the "global war on terror" an adequate expression of America's universal mission or a dangerous caricature of it?

9. Ernest L. Tuveson, *Redeemer Nation: The Idea of America's Millennial Role* (Chicago/London: University of Chicago Press, 1968).
10. Jürgen Moltmann, *The Coming of God*, p. 169.

Messianic Symbols

There will be ample reason at a later point to reflect on the question of whether messianic claims can be compatible with the growing need of the nations of the earth to "work it out together," to use that familiar expression that suggests resolving conflicts in an amicable way. At this point in my attempt to understand the self-concept of "America," I find it urgent to look at how the political messianism of the "redeemer nation" is communicated to almost 300 million citizens. What makes it possible that women and men of the world's most diverse backgrounds, regions, traditions, and cultures should regard themselves as Americans? What is it that promotes this rapid identification with the messianic "America"? Obviously, this cannot be achieved solely by the public discourse as exemplified in the presidents' inaugural addresses or state of the union messages. One answer may be found in the symbolic communication that seems to bond the American people into a unity of sentiment in, for example, the American flag and two of the most important national feast days, Thanksgiving and Memorial Day.

Back in 1965, during my first stay in the United States, I was amazed and perplexed to see that there was a flag in every church, in most cases in the nave, that is, in the most sacred space. Had I not been taught that the strict separation of church and state was one of America's special achievements and inviolable principles? The Constitution permits the establishment of no state church (as in Scandinavian countries) and no church tax (as in Germany, Austria, and Switzerland). And yet there was the flag in every church! A friend told me that, during the Iraq War of 2003, "The Star-Spangled Banner," America's national anthem, was sung in each worship service of his church. How could the flag and the cross stand together so congenially?

When I arrived in America in 1965, it had been only twenty years in Germany since the nationalistic frenzy of the Nazis. Therefore, the expression of patriotic sentiments was highly suspect to me. It would have been unthinkable to place the flag of the Federal Republic of Germany in one of our churches. And it is still unthinkable. Yet, at the same time, there does exist a close institutional relationship between the *Landeskirchen,* the territorial Catholic and Protestant churches, and the German national state. Among other things, the German national government acts as the collector of the *Kirchensteur* (church tax) and underwrites the cost of religious instruction within the public schools. In recent times it has become a habit for winners in international sports events to wrap themselves in their national flags, and German athletes are no exception. But it is extremely rare for people in Germany to fly a flag in front of their homes.

In the summer of 1966, I worked for three months in a parish in Philadelphia. The minister of the church, his wife, and their five children spent their vacation at the family's summer house in Vermont, and they invited me to join them for a weekend. This turned out to be highly enjoyable for many reasons. But there was one moment that I found perplexing: in the morning, before breakfast, the grandfather assembled his five grandchildren at the swimming pool. While one of them had the honor of hoisting the flag, the others stood in line, their right hands over their hearts, as they saluted the "Stars and Stripes."

A trivial event, to be sure; but I thought, "This is how it begins." The identification with the symbol of "America, the beautiful" begins right next to the swimming pool at home. It starts in the homes of wonderful people, in loving and caring families; it continues in the schools and summer camps; and it is a "natural" part of sports events and public celebrations. Thus the flag becomes a strand in the fabric of patriotic feelings as it does perhaps nowhere else, as Samuel Huntington confirms: "Although no exact comparative statistics exist, it seems probable that in almost no other country is the flag so pervasively present and so central to national identity."[11] And as Edward W. Said, the great intellectual of Palestinian origin, has said: "I know of no other country in which the flowing flag is such a central icon. You see it everywhere. . . . In a singular way, the flag embodies the self-image of the nation. It stands for heroic perseverance and the conviction to be surrounded by unworthy enemies."[12]

11. Samuel Huntington, *Who Are We? America's Great Debate* (London: Free Press, 2004), p. 128.

12. Edward Said, "The Other America," *Al Ahram* (Egypt), March 20-26, 2003: http://weekly.ahram.org.eg/2003/630/focus.htm (accessed Oct. 12, 2005).

This is good, isn't it? Or is it not that good after all? Perhaps I am too skeptical because of my German background. But my question remains: When does a positive symbol turn into a negative one? After the terrorist attacks of September 11, 2001, the United States was almost drowning in flags. I think that, to some extent, this was a demonstration of reassurance and commitment in the face of those shocking attacks. On the other hand, however, the rallying around the flag was a way of suppressing unpleasant criticism and a means of preparing the American people emotionally for war against the terrorists.

While the flag is America's constantly visible symbol, the national holidays are recurrent rituals in the yearly cycle. Thanksgiving Day dates back to the first celebration of the Pilgrims, who gave thanks to God for having survived in the wilderness. (It was soon overlooked that they had survived largely because of the active support of the indigenous "Indian" peoples around them.) Thanksgiving became the symbolic expression of the nation that is aware of its providential calling and committed to resist the threatening pressures from the wilderness. To be sure, most Americans celebrate Thanksgiving as a family affair. As such, it is the moment to appreciate the sustaining networks of family and friends. But the old message is a part of it still, not least in the rustic elements of the great Thanksgiving dinner.

Memorial Day has a different character. It was inspired in part by the 1863 ceremony in remembrance of those who had fallen during the Battle of Gettysburg. Abraham Lincoln's famous "Gettysburg Address" attempted to give meaning to the deaths of those Civil War victims: "[W]e here highly resolve that these dead shall not have died in vain; that this nation under God shall have a new birth of freedom, and that this government of the people, by the people, and for the people shall not perish from the earth." Again, these classic words reveal the political messianism of the "American experiment." The rebirth of liberty is to be gained by the sacrificial death of those who died — and continued to die — on the battlefield. This interpretation invokes Christ's sacrificial death for the redemption of the world. Moreover, when Abraham Lincoln was murdered on Good Friday of 1865, his death also acquired sacrificial meaning, which was popularized by Walt Whitman in poems and lectures after the war. It seemed to Whitman and to many others that Lincoln, too, had given his life for the well-being — indeed the immortality — of the nation. The links between Christ's sacrificial death for the redemption of humankind and the death of American soldiers for the redemption of the world appeared to be obvious. The "nation under God" thus regards itself as God's sacrificial agent for the nations of the earth: those who fall in this struggle are the martyrs for the better world to come.

While Thanksgiving Day has become a symbol for the "family values" on which the life of each American — and any other human being — depends, Memorial Day is the symbolic expression of America's civil religion, one in which the sacrificial messianic role of this "nation under God" is invoked again and again. President George W. Bush said the following in his 2005 Memorial Day address at Arlington Cemetery: "Looking across the field, we see the scale of heroism and sacrifice. . . . All stood to protect America. . . . Because of the sacrifice of our men and women in uniform, two terror regimes are gone forever, freedom is on the march, and America is more secure."[13]

Obviously, symbolic celebrations function to reaffirm and to reestablish the commitment of a country's citizenry to the goals their leaders set before them. Ceremonies such as laying a wreath on the Tomb of the Unknown Soldier in Arlington Cemetery on Memorial Day are necessary to deepen the symbolic communication among Americans and to affirm their acceptance of a war in Iraq that has become increasingly unpopular.

But I don't wish to overlook the fact that Memorial Day is far less popular than Thanksgiving. Furthermore, it is important to keep in mind that these two national holidays are not the only national moments of ceremony in the United States. Among the others, Martin Luther King Day, established by the U.S. Congress and signed into law in 1986 by President Reagan, deserves special mention. Preceded by years of struggle for its passage, this commemoration became a symbolic expression of America's ongoing struggle for the civil liberties of each cit-

---

13. George W. Bush, "President Commemorates Memorial Day at Arlington Cemetery, May 30, 2005" (White House release: www.whitehouse.gov/news/releases/2005/05/20050530.html [accessed Oct. 20, 2005]).

izen. As such, it is an example of a creative diversity within U.S. society; it brings fresh and critical aspects to the symbolic discourse that holds the country together. At the same time, we should not overlook the fact that Martin Luther King Day has not yet attained the prominence of the two ceremonial days already mentioned. And though it was established as a federal holiday, some states were slow to adopt the observance.

Chosen People and Chosen Triumph

What happens when America regards itself as the elected instrument of the Lord of history? And what is the consequence of granting to those who die for this "mission" the status of martyrs? Such a nation is bound to claim that it is always on the side of the good and the just and, therefore, innocent of any blood that is shed. Moltmann quotes John Adams, who wrote in a letter to Thomas Jefferson: "Many hundred years must roll away before we shall be corrupted. Our pure, virtuous, public spirited, federative republic will last forever, govern the globe and introduce the perfection of man."[14] And Thomas Jefferson, too, spoke of the young republic as the "innocent nation in a wicked world."[15] In those days it must have sounded right, especially if one compared the young settler communities of the New World with the feudal states of Europe and their deceitful power politics. In those early years it must have seemed easy for those who had escaped the vanity and corruption of "old Europe" to see themselves as young and pure, as the chosen people with a calling to do the Lord's work and to usher in the final stage of history and the "perfection of man."

As long as the fledgling United States, under its Articles of Confederation, was powerless, such claims to innocence were fairly harmless. But this changed dramatically as the United States began to conquer the territories to the West of the original colonies. As early as 1817, the Monroe Doctrine had established the claim that other countries must

14. Moltmann, *Coming of God,* p. 171.
15. Moltmann, *Coming of God,* p. 171.

refrain from colonizing on the American continents, North or South, which were declared to be the U.S. sphere of influence. While the United States would not interfere with the affairs of the states in Europe, it expected European powers to stay away from the American continent. The Monroe Doctrine was a political expression of what I would call the discovery of greatness. The Puritan "errand into the wilderness" had eventually revealed the truly tremendous and tempting potential of the New (and much larger) World. Here were the open spaces for the messianic progress of the chosen people.

By 1850, it had become customary to say that it was America's "manifest destiny" to take possession of the land. The "Wild West" was to become the Garden of Eden. The circuit riders of the Methodist Church were out there to establish the ways of God among the lawless and the heathen. The great railroad lines opened up the country and made it easier for people to go west in their search for land and gold. To those who were part of this great sweep across the American continent, their appetite for conquest seemed unstoppable and, in religious terms, divinely ordained and blessed. So it must have become almost natural for them to consider those who opposed this great movement not only as their worldly enemies but also as enemies of divine destiny. The indigenous peoples, the "Indians," were not only heathen people who were to be converted and then incorporated into the body politic (what had largely happened in Latin America); but also they stood, as it were, in God's way, and thus it was unavoidable that they had to be put out of the way.

Manifest Destiny became a concept by which the excesses of conquest could be excused. The concept helped to justify the Indian Wars, as well as the Spanish-American War of 1898, and, last but not least, the purchase and prolonged military occupation of the Philippines.[16]

16. President McKinley explained the reasons why he ordered the annexation of the Philippines in the following way: "When I realized that the Philippines had dropped into our lap I did not know what to do with them. I sought counsel from all sides . . . but got little help. . . . I walked the floor of the White House night after night until midnight; and I am not ashamed to tell you, gentlemen, that I went down on my knees and prayed Almighty God for light and guidance more than one night. And one night late it came to me this way — I don't know how it was, but it came: (1) That we could not give

Manifest Destiny is a precarious justification because it helps to establish a dualistic understanding of history. It sets the "chosen people" against those who are not. It allows an all-too-easy distinction between "right" and "wrong," between the "good guys" and the "bad guys," indeed, between "good" and "evil." What I find particularly precarious is the implicit claim of innocence. It makes it difficult for the victors to see the sufferings on the enemy's side, and it makes it easy for the victors to deny their own guilt.[17]

I can highlight what the messianic claim can do to the identity of a nation by noting the observations of the American psychotherapist Vamik D. Volkan.[18] He shows that decisive historical experiences and images can have a formative impact on the self-understanding of peoples. For the Serbian people, for example, their defeat at the hands of the advancing Ottoman Empire in 1389 has served as the hermeneutical key determining their historical calling and mission. To be sure, the

---

them back to Spain — that would be cowardly and dishonorable; (2) that we could not turn them over to France or Germany — our commercial rivals in the Orient — that would be bad business and discreditable; (3) that we could not leave them to themselves — they were unfit for self-government . . . and (4) that there was nothing left for us to do but to take them all, and to educate the Filipinos, and uplift and civilize and Christian-ize them, and by God's grace do the very best for them, as our fellow-men for whom Christ also died. And I went to bed and went to sleep, and slept soundly, and the next morning I sent for the chief engineer of the War Department (our map-maker), and told him to put the Philippines on the map of the United States . . . and there they are, and there they will stay while I am President!" (General James Rusling, "Interview with President William McKinley," *The Christian Advocate,* Feb. 22, 1903, p. 17; reprinted in Daniel Schirmer and Stephen Rosskamm Shalom, eds., *The Philippines Reader* [Boston: South End Press, 1987], pp. 22-23).

17. Robert Jewett and John S. Lawrence say: "Shielded by the idea of remote-controlled wrath, Americans found it virtually impossible to assess blame for genocide. When one surveys the long series of massacres, reaching from King Philip's War in 1675-1676 to the Battle of Wounded Knee in 1890, Americans virtually never alleged or confessed individual responsibility for them. Well-publicized excesses such as the Sand Creek Massacre were occasionally condemned, but the responsible policy-makers were never brought to trial. By and large, the saints felt as guiltless in those engagements as Daniel felt about the fate of his enemies in the lions' den" (*Captain America and the Crusade Against Evil* [Grand Rapids: Eerdmans, 2003], p. 178).

18. Vamik D. Volkan has worked with people in severe conflict situations — for instance, in the Baltics, former Yugoslavia, and South Africa.

Battle of the Kosovo in 1389 was for them a traumatic experience because it established their subservient status within the Muslim Ottoman Empire.[19] But it became much more than one tragic incident in their history; the Serbs turned it into the one and only trauma by which they interpreted themselves and their nation — their raison d'être. Volkan calls this hermeneutical process "chosen trauma."[20] He does not deny that a traumatic event has occurred; but, he points out, when that process of "choosing" such an event serves as the sole interpretive key for the self-image of an entire nation, it becomes the exclusive point of orientation for the nation's identity. This implies that other historical experiences cannot be integrated adequately, and the "chosen trauma" determines the official narrative of a nation and hence its political options. In the case of Serbia, this disposition provided its leaders with the pretext to launch the civil war for control of Kosovo in 1989: they explicitly referred to the six-hundredth anniversary of the Battle of the Kosovo.

Volkan goes on to show that there are other nations who base their identity not on a chosen trauma but on a "chosen triumph": they "choose" a positive original experience to serve as the dominating hermeneutical key for their self-understanding and thus for their political options. Volkan says that the founding myths of the United States have become something like a "chosen triumph."[21] "Mine eyes have seen the glory of the coming of the Lord," the opening line of "The Battle Hymn of the Republic," identifies God's glory with the glorious progress of America. Since the nation is seen to have been

19. Vamik Volkan, *Blind Trust: Large Groups and Their Leaders in Times of Crisis and Terror* (Charlottesville, VA: Pitchstone Publishing, 2004), pp. 50-52.

20. Volkan, *Blind Trust,* pp. 47ff.

21. In the German edition of *Blind Trust,* Volkan points out that the first Thanksgiving of 1621 was by no means the great feast that it later became. He also mentions that among the Pilgrim fathers there were people of rather dubious motives and that the land on which they settled had already been cleared by the indigenous people who inhabited that region (Volkan, *Das Versagen der Diplomatie. Zur Psychoanalyse nationaler, ethnischer und religiöser Konflikte,* 2nd ed. [Gießen: Psychosozial-Verlag, 2000], pp. 71f.). His information is derived from Robert A. Furman, "The Pilgrims: Myth and Reality," University of Virginia Health Systems: http://www.healthsystem.virginia.edu/internet/csmhi/furman.cfm. (accessed Dec. 10, 2005).

founded under God's providence, and since its successes have been won by divine guidance, it can only envision its course ahead in triumphant ways.

Hence the messianic experiment carries the marks of a "chosen triumph." Again, one cannot deny that the United States has experienced great triumphs. The point is that, when a nation sees its great victories in the image of a divinely ordained triumph, it prevents itself from perceiving the impact of these victories on others. This helps explain why, in the wake of 9/11, so many American citizens, including their president, simply could not understand why there was so much hatred of the United States around the world. It also helps us understand why its citizens have so casually accepted the new mission that has been officially designated as the "global war on terrorism."[22]

State Church and Civil Religion

In March 2003, the British Catholic journal *The Tablet* published an article by Clifford Langley that compares the relationship of President Bush and Prime Minister Tony Blair with respect to the churches of their respective countries. Both leaders say that they are committed Christians. President Bush openly uses religious language and regularly closes his speeches by invoking God's blessings on the United States (even though the First Amendment of the Constitution has established a strict separation of church and state). Many European observers find this presidential expression of piety perplexing. It has not escaped them that many mainline churches in the United States have openly — and also in the name of God — criticized the president for going to war against Iraq, while other churches, mostly of a more conservative character, have praised Bush as God's servant because he wages war against the terrorists. Indeed, the United Methodist Church, the Protestant de-

22. See "The Global War on Terrorism" (White House Release, December 2001: http://www.whitehouse.gov/news/releases/2001/12/100dayreport.html [accessed Nov. 20, 2005]).

nomination to which both President Bush and Vice President Cheney belong, has repudiated their Iraq war policies.[23] So what kind of "God" is it that the president and the various Christian churches are talking about? From afar, it looks as though there is a rather intimate relationship between state and church, more intimate than warranted by the Constitution.

Langley contrasts this observation with the situation in England, which has an established church (the Anglican Communion), of which the prime minister must be a member. At the same time, the election of the Archbishop of Canterbury must be agreed upon by the prime minister; and the Archbishop himself is a member of the House of Lords. Yet, despite this close link between state and church, there are, of course, a number of "free churches" in Britain. Archbishop Rowan Williams has been a stout critic of Blair's joining the United States in the war against Iraq. So Langley concludes that, if a person from another planet were to observe Bush and Blair, she would have to conclude that, while Bush has made religion into an affair of the state, Blair is required to keep religion and politics clearly apart.

You don't have to come from another planet to get it wrong. Outside observers often overlook the fact that the political culture of the United States is based less on the Christian churches and more on what Robert Bellah has called "civil religion."[24] To be sure, America's civil religion draws heavily on Christian images and symbols, but it can easily include references to Judaism, Islam, and other religious traditions. A good example was the "worship service" at the National Cathedral in Washington, D.C., on September 16, 2001. It was designed to be the official American response to the terrorist attacks of September 11 against the Twin Towers in New York and the Pentagon (as well as the apparently failed attack aimed at the White House). Representatives of various religious faiths had a part in it; the president spoke

25. John Dart, "Church Leaders Oppose Attack on Iraq," *Christian Century,* Sept. 11, 2002, p. 14. Segments of the Methodist Church have since called for withdrawal from Iraq through "A Call to Repentance and Peace with Justice" (United Methodist Church: http://www.umc.org/site/c.gjJTJbMUIuE/b.1174097/k.FD54/A_Call_to_Repentance_and_Peace_with_Justice.htm [accessed Dec. 10, 2005]).

24. Robert N. Bellah, "Civil Religion in America," *Daedalus* 96, no. 1 (1967): 1-21.

from the pulpit; "The Battle Hymn of the Republic" was sung — all the ingredients of a religious ceremony were in place.

I don't wish to be misunderstood. I fully understand that the executive branch of the U.S. government felt that it was necessary to unite the nation through an act of remembrance and commitment. What I wish to illustrate here is the fact that this ritual in the National Cathedral was not a worship service or any other kind of church affair; it was more clearly an expression of America's civil religion. One can conclude, I think, that this civil religion has become the religion of the state — in other words, a national faith — with a president officiating as its high priest. This is a stark way of putting it, but it explains a phenomenon that has been puzzling many European observers. Though both President Bush and Prime Minister Blair have been roundly criticized by leaders of the Christian churches in the United States and the United Kingdom, the difference is that Bush does not need to be bothered by it at all. He does not need the support of the churches because he has the "national religion" — or civil religion — to rely on. This "religion" has acquired its own traditions, its own rituals, relics, symbols, and "holy places."

Below is a statement that Swiss theologian Lukas Vischer found posted in a Catholic church in New York City:

Pray for our Military — A Prayer for America

We are America,
the heart of a world seeking
freedom and peace. We are
the East and the West, the North and the South —
one people embracing many. We are a legacy
of courage with a destiny of greatness.
We are history and prophecy, liberty and home,
refuge and vision.
So we lift up our light as a beacon of hope
with this prayer to our God and Creator:
Make us a people who care and comfort.
Let us reach out a welcoming hand
to the homeless, the helpless, the hungry.

> Let us fulfill God's great plan
> for our land. Let our gift to the nations be love.[25]

This text embodies both the appealing and the appalling qualities of America's national religion. It speaks of offering "a welcoming hand to the homeless, the helpless, the hungry." It speaks of "love" as America's "gift to the nations." There can be no doubt that a great deal of generous love goes out from the United States to people in need throughout the world; but this disguises the fact that the United States has also brought destruction and war to large parts of the world. This "prayer" does not reveal a trace of humility. Instead, it resounds with the triumphant and naive self-aggrandizement of the "we" as the "heart of the world." The hubris and self-righteousness in phrases such as "we are history and prophecy, liberty and home, refuge and vision" is hard for outsiders to swallow; and I'm certain that many Americans are ashamed of this triumphalism as well.

Abraham Lincoln, in his Gettysburg Address, spoke of a "nation under God." He knew well that God must always remain the Reality/ Mystery that transcends even the greatest exploits of nations. A "prayer" such as the one above appears to have lost the dimension of being "under"; instead, it puts "God" and "America" at an equal level. It pretends to know "God's great plan" and claims to "fulfill" it — with Lincoln's added guarantee "that government of the people, by the people, for the people, shall not perish from the earth."

I write this with a sad heart, for I am a citizen of a nation that has also sent her soldiers to war with the proud slogan "For God and Fatherland." Clifford Langley is a citizen of a nation, Great Britain, in which the Bishop of London, Arthur Winington-Ingram, called World War I a "holy war." That was the title of one of his sermons, in which he proclaimed: "This is a Holy War. We are on the side of Christianity against anti-Christ."[26] Many Europeans of my generation have had enough of this kind of "holiness" and this kind of "God." As we look

---

25. In a letter dated Sept. 10, 2004.

26. Alan Wilkinson, *The Church of England and the First World War* (London: SPCK, 1978), p. 253.

at the Holocaust and the other excesses of fascism, as well as the gulags in communist countries, we are fatigued by every kind of triumphalist, messianic claim to purify our world. There is hardly a family in Europe that has not lost members in the bloody excesses of the twentieth century.

I was five years old when my father returned from his five years of "service" in the Wehrmacht. I remember the first question I put to him: *Wann gibt es wieder Krieg?* ("When will there be war again?") And I remember his answer: *Nie wieder!* ("Never again!") Of course, my question was naive, and his answer was not true. But the fear behind my question and the shock behind his answer were utterly real. So is the recognition that national-triumphalist ideologies of all kinds are foolish and bound to end in disaster.

So I am left with questions: Who and what is God in America? What effect does America's national religion have on the ways it uses its considerable power the world over? How are the Christian churches to disentangle themselves from a national religion that appears to justify even the gravest political errors? What kind of dialogue is necessary within and between Christian communities — from left to right — to discover what Jesus Christ means for them today? A lively debate is underway in the United States already.[27] But before I offer my observations, I would like to turn to a religious phenomenon that Europeans find most perplexing. I refer to the apocalyptic literature of the *Left Behind* series.

27. For a vivid example of this debate, see "End Times and End Games: Is Scripture Being *Left Behind*?" *Reflections,* Yale Divinity School (Spring 2005).

CHAPTER 2

End-Time Religion in America

—⚭—

Most Europeans, including the French (!), would consider Americans their more-or-less distant cousins: on both sides of the Atlantic there is a big "we," and we all take that family kind of relationship for granted. Basically, it means that we all share the same values and cultural traditions. Despite all other apparent differences, our politicians keep repeating this fundamental belief. Most visibly, such a belief in unity provides a foundation for the privileged relationship between Great Britain and the United States. But German politicians also keep insisting that the traditional friendship between our two countries has much deeper roots than the close alliance that was forged after World War II. Immigration from Europe to the United States, as well as cross-pollination in the past century, has meant that there are intimate relationships between the peoples in the United States and those in Europe. In spite of the internal divisions, Christianity — or what might more adequately be called the Judaeo-Christian tradition — may well be the closest link.

It is important to remember this profound common heritage. But that should not prevent us from acknowledging that the divisions within the Western world and within this Judaeo-Christian tradition are growing. In the first chapter I referred to the fact that the messianic components of America's "national religion" are not shared by most Europeans. As a matter of fact, Europeans don't even understand them. This lack of understanding reflects a kind of disenchantment with the quasi-religious political ideologies that have ravaged European countries. Consequently, the widespread secularization in "old Europe" can also be seen as a spiritual exhaustion. People are weary of the ideological "battles of the spirit" and suspicious of political leaders who advocate a new search for "the soul of Europe."

As a Christian theologian, I am especially concerned about the growing divisions within the Christian communities of Europe and the United States. Certainly, there continue to be close contacts between the Protestant churches here and the mainline churches in the United States (I assume that the same is true for the Roman Catholic Church and the Orthodox churches). But this is mostly a link between churches with "liberal" positions. It leaves out the growing evangelical and charismatic Christian communities. There is nothing in Europe that compares to the "Bible belt" in the United States. Our academic theologians and church leaders do not know how to relate to the brothers and sisters of the religious right, and I have the impression that this is equally true of the liberal churches in the United States. Nor do conservative Christian leaders in America care to understand the specific experiences that have impacted Protestant churches in Europe. In addition to the traditional differences in theology and worship, contemporary Protestantism is deeply divided along the "conservative"/ "liberal" divide.[1]

Left Behind is a telling example: a best-selling book series in America that has not caused a ripple in the life of the churches in Europe. The original twelve volumes of the series, written by Tim LaHaye and Jerry Jenkins, have evolved into an enormous industry (a series for children, two movies, music programs, PC games, and all the other "franchise" products that accompany a smashing success) —

---

1. One prominent theologian who works to overcome this silence is Jim Wallis in *God's Politics: Why the Right Gets It Wrong and the Left Doesn't Get It* (San Francisco: HarperSanFrancisco, 2005). Yale Divinity School discusses some of these problems in the Spring 2005 issue of *Reflections,* entitled "End Times and End Games: Is Scripture Being *Left Behind?*"

none of which can be found in Europe.[2] To be sure, this division tells us much about the spiritual state of Europeans. If one simply looks at the bestseller lists, Europeans are much more interested in what happens to young Harry Potter than they are in what happens to Christ. This is a phenomenon that Christian churches on the European continent should be concerned about.

Yet this is not the line I want to follow here. Instead, my question is: Why are productions such as the *Left Behind* series "indigenous" to a large segment of life in the United States? Are they an outgrowth of religious traditions that have shaped the United States more intensely than they have shaped the host countries from which many of their citizens have come? As everywhere in this book, I remind my readers that I am describing how these matters are understood from the European side of the Atlantic.

Left Behind: Remarks on the History of Apocalyptic Scenarios

There is no need to relate in great detail the content of this twelve-volume series. It purports to be a narrative illustration of what the Bible, especially the book of Revelation, says about the last years of the world that culminate in the Second Coming of Jesus Christ. According to this reading of Scripture, the crucial time will begin with the "Rapture," that is, the lifting up of the true believers into the clouds of heaven, sparing them the seven years of "tribulations." During those years the Antichrist will appear and will manage to unite all the world's people under one religion and one government. He will guide the vast armies of the world against the small underground resistance army of Christians (to which exactly 144,000 converted Jews will belong). Satan will be defeated, captured, and cast into a pit by the extra-terrestrial forces of Jesus Christ, who will then set up the latter's

2. The same is true for Hal Lindsey's *The Late Great Planet Earth*, which first appeared in 1970 and went through many editions (with interesting alterations). Although it has been an American blockbuster, eventually selling more than 20 million copies, there was no German edition until *Alter Planet Erde Wohin?* appeared in 1991, which created no stir.

thousand-year reign of peace (before Satan is allowed to have another go at it).

It is difficult to ascertain whether the vast readership of this series of books agrees with every detail of it. I imagine that many people consume the books just as they consume other science-fiction novels. Perhaps what we are seeing here is a new brand of "religious fiction." The books' fixation on apocalyptic end-time scenarios is certainly not shared by all evangelical Christians. In fact, there has been quite a bit of criticism of the books from among evangelicals.[3] Nevertheless, it is remarkable that so many millions of Americans should be attracted to this kind of literature — even if it is only an "entertaining fantasy" for many of them.

I have noted that this series is not the first attempt to write the story of humankind's final days, nor will it be the last. For example, Tyndale House, the publishing company that has made so much money from the *Left Behind* novels, has already begun — in the manner of the *Star Wars* films — to publish a *Countdown to the Rapture* "prequels" series. Lindsey's *The Late Great Planet Earth* (1970) was among its forerunners in its conception of the Rapture. But, even before Lindsey, there have been many attempts to come to terms with the nagging questions concerning the end of history as it relates to the ultimate goal of life on earth.

As a matter of fact, this question originated in biblical times and has been a preoccupation of theologians and artists ever since. It is hardly an exaggeration to say that the book of Revelation has had a more pervasive and troublesome influence on the Christian world than any other biblical book. One need only refer to the images of the "City of God" or the "New Jerusalem" or the "grapes of wrath" to appreciate its vast impact on Christian spirituality, not to mention religious art, throughout the centuries. Jürgen Moltmann has provided a superb overview of the ways in which thinking about "the last days" — the

---

3. For a detailed analysis of how readers experience *Left Behind,* see Amy Johnson Frykholm, *Rapture Culture: Left Behind in Evangelical America* (New York: Oxford University Press, 2004); for the array of critical disagreement among Christians, see Bruce D. Forbes and Jeanne Halgren Kilde, eds., *Rapture, Revelation, and the End Time: Exploring the Left Behind Series* (New York: Palgrave Macmillan, 2004).

eschatological aspect of the Christian faith — has had its expression in the early decades of Christianity, in the Middle Ages, and also in modern times.[4] He demonstrates that there was a heavy emphasis on "messianic eschatology" in the post-Reformation period. He refers to English, Dutch, Italian, and German sources to show that Christian groups were increasingly fascinated by the idea that the kingdom of God was a reality unfolding itself in concrete time. People who held these electrifying convictions would often be the ones leaving Europe for the New World, because that anticipated world appeared to possess all the marks of the kingdom.[5]

But not all of them did. There were sizeable groups of people who stayed behind and studied the apocalyptic texts in the light of their time and their specific experiences. Two examples may illustrate this. During the Napoleonic Wars, which brought so much havoc to the countries in central Europe, some rural communities near the university town of Tübingen came to the conclusion that they must be living in the end time and that, surely, Napoleon, with his unaccountable successes, must be the Antichrist. They were equally certain that Christ would have to come again in the land of the Christian tzar of Russia because he had taken up the valiant fight against the apostate from France. Finally, they believed that Christ would surely return to earth at Mount Ararat, because that was where Noah's Ark had come to land.

As the leaders of the small rural communities considered all these things, they concluded that it would be a sign of genuine discipleship to await Christ's Second Coming at the foot of Mount Ararat in Armenia. Consequently, several thousand men, women, and children left their villages in Germany and set out on the long trek to Mount Ararat — singing hymns of expectation as they left their homes. But after only a few days the troubles began, and most of those making the pilgrimage died on the way. Only a very small group made it all the way to the foot of Mount Ararat; and had not the Basel Mission provided some means

4. Jürgen Moltmann, *Coming of God,* pp. 129-255.

5. An example is Johann Georg Rapp (1757-1847), who awaited the return of Christ in the year 1829 at Harmony, Pennsylvania. See Eberhard Fritz, *Radikaler Pietismus in Württemberg* (Epfendorf, Germany: Bibliotheca Academica Verlag, 2003), pp. 201-56.

to get them settled, they would all have perished. Some few villages of these pilgrims continued to exist up until World War II, only to be exiled by Stalin to faraway Kazakhstan. And there they have vanished.[6]

The other example is of the famous theologian Johann Albrecht Bengel (1687-1752), who was an influential figure during the German pietistic awakenings. His studies of the book of Revelation led him to predict that the world would be coming to its end on June 18, 1836. On "the day after," that is, on June 19, 1836, when nothing had happened, the pietistic communities were in profound commotion. This had a sobering effect: Christian leaders began to realize that it would make more sense to leave the coming of the kingdom to God alone. True faith in God would restrain a person from the calculation of dates, and it came to be understood that the end time might or might not happen within linear calendar time. Since God was the Lord of time, time might undergo profound transformation.[7]

What took place in Germany was a subtle change away from millennialist calculations to a spiritual or internal millennialism that saw the coming of the kingdom of God in the slow amelioration of the state of human affairs. This transformation was already reflected in the writings of Johann Amos Comenius, the last bishop of the persecuted Moravian Brethren (1592-1670), and it became an ingredient of humanism and Enlightenment thought. One can see traces of Comenius's interests in the influential writer and philosopher Gotthold Ephraim Lessing (1729-1781). Both were convinced that the kingdom of God would be advanced by working for educational reforms. In the words of Jürgen Moltmann: "The kingdom of God is coming, but it will not be the result of an apocalyptic revolution brought about by God; it will come through the growth of reason and morality among human beings."[8] The preoccupation with end-time scenarios in Germany disappeared as a widely popular phenomenon and survived only in very small circles.[9]

6. See Georg Leibbrandt, *Die Auswanderung nach Russland, 1816-1823* (Stuttgart: Ausland und Heimat Verlag, 1928).
7. Moltmann, *Coming of God*, pp. 145, 199-200.
8. Moltmann, p. 189.
9. Moltmann, pp. 156-59, 187-88.

Not so in other countries. There the "prophetic search" continued. Theologians and evangelists kept looking for ways to read the signs of the times. For them, Johann Bengel had simply gotten the facts wrong — not to mention the pitiful communities near Tübingen, which had obviously messed it all up.[10] Among the theologians who claimed to have found the right key to salvation's history was John Nelson Darby, a son of Irish aristocrats who was born in 1800. He became a minister of the Church of England, but he broke away from that body and established the Plymouth Brethren. The main reason Darby turned his back on the Anglican Communion was that it tolerated persons who were not converted. The "Brethren" were to be a community of men and women committed to purity in faith, doctrine, and life. As a matter of course, this rigorousness of purity provoked many splits; but "Darbyism" continued. The majority of its adherents now live in the United States, with some small communities in Germany.[11]

Darby's main influence on later generations, however, was to be his eschatology — that is, his "doctrine of the last things." It was based on the assumption that every word of Holy Scripture has been inspired by God, and thus the will and purpose of God has to be contained in this book. Concerning the history of God's salvific work for humankind, the prophetic and apocalyptic passages of the Bible must surely make up God's "road map" to the kingdom. Darby's reading of Scripture gave him to believe that world history had gone through seven "dispensations," and that the end of the seventh — and thus the beginning of the apocalyptic end-time "tribulations" — was at hand.[12]

Obviously, Darby was not the only one to propose such ideas. The famous evangelist D. L. Moody shared his end-time urgency, as did

10. The American social psychologists Festinger, Riecken, and Schachter investigated a similar phenomenon in their book *When Prophecy Fails* (1957), which discusses an end-time group in America that suffered from failing predictions.

11. The leading representative of Darbyism in Germany was Carl Brockhaus, who met Darby in 1854. Many Darbyist "Brethren" communities joined Baptist churches. Today there are some 35,000 Darbyists in Germany. For further details, see O. Eggenberger, *"Darbyisten," Religion in Geschichte und Gegenwart*, 3rd ed., vol. 2 (Tübingen: Mohr, 1986), pp. 40ff.

12. Craig C. Hill, *In God's Time: The Bible and the Future* (Grand Rapids: Eerdmans, 2002), pp. 200-201.

C. I. Scofield, whose influential *Scofield Reference Bible* (1909) was studied — and accepted — by a vast readership. Incidentally, it is also interesting to note that, parallel to the spreading of Darbyism in the later decades of the nineteenth century, three other communities with clear apocalyptical messages came into existence in America: the Seventh-day Adventists, the Mormons, and the Jehovah's Witnesses.

One of the central problems in all these attempts to properly read the signs of the times and bring them into accord with the biblical basis is this: according to their reading of St. Paul's Letter to the Romans (especially Rom. 11:25ff.), the Jews would return to their promised land before Christ would come back in glory. So when the state of Israel was founded in 1948, many end-time prophets regarded this as the unmistakable historical proof that the final hour was near.

Working with "historical proofs" gives this kind of speculative thinking about biblical interpretation a "scientific" appearance. But this insistence on proofs and data actually reveals a decidedly modern approach: biblical texts are handled in the same way that physical or chemical data are used by natural scientists. Both analyze their materials in order to arrive at clear scientific conclusions. I find it important to highlight this modern approach in works such as *Left Behind* in order to challenge claims by their authors that their story is nothing other than a clear and simple narrative of the biblical message. Theirs is a *biblicism* that has more in common with historical materialism and pre-Einstein scientific optimism than with the diverse spiritualities of the biblical texts.[13]

Essentially, we are faced with an urgent hermeneutical problem. How are the biblical texts to be interpreted? And this is by no means a problem for Americans only. It is an international and, if you will, an ecumenical concern: How do we read the Bible? Who is Jesus Christ for us today? It is deplorable that there are only a few academic theologians who are prepared to accept this challenge. The experts work-

13. Adela Y. Collins says: "The whole dispensationalist approach is a kind of fundamentalist, conservative appropriation of the Enlightenment in a way. The dispensationalists adopted the values of rationality and systematic thought from the Enlightenment. They tried to read the Bible as a unity in a new, highly rationalistic way" (*Reflections*, p. 12).

ing in related fields do not wish to busy themselves with phenomena such as the *Left Behind* productions. For them, this debate was over a long time ago, largely because of the rise of historical criticism and related methods of interpreting the biblical texts.[14] While this may be true for them, the debate is not over for millions of untrained women and men all over the world.

Why bother so much? Wouldn't it be wiser to let this "doom boom" run its course until it suffocates in its own unfulfilled dreams? My response is this: it is too dangerous a phenomenon to allow it to run wild, for the following three reasons.

Apocalyptic Scenarios Are an Interreligious Reality

We are faced with an interreligious reality. The scary thing is that we are not dealing with Christian apocalypticism alone. There are Islamic versions that adopt the same structure, often borrowing liberally from Christian commentaries, albeit with entirely opposite interpretations. As David Cook points out, Islam, too, has apocalyptic traditions that go back to biblical sources; they have given rise to influential end-time scenarios that circulate widely in the Islamic world.[15] In Islam the Antichrist is called the *dajjal*. He will appear at the end of time to seduce Muslims and to draw them away from their true faith. In fact, the *dajjal* is also accountable for the depravities and abominations of the modern time. For instance, he controls Hollywood's film industry! Islam has even enlisted Jesus — this time as a Muslim savior — in the role of returning to defeat the *dajjal* and to pave the way for the Mahdi, the Muslim messiah, who will then establish his reign of jus-

14. An interesting example: John Polkinghorne and Michael Welker, eds., *The End of the World and the Ends of God: Science and Theology on Eschatology* (Harrisburg, PA: Trinity Press International, 2000).

15. David Cook, "Muslim Fears of the Year 2000," *The Middle East Quarterly* (June 1998): 51-62; an online version of this article is posted by the Middle East Forum: http://www.meforum.org/article/397 (accessed Oct. 20, 2005). Cook more recently published a book-length survey, *Contemporary Muslim Apocalyptic Literature* (Syracuse, NY: Syracuse University Press, 2005).

tice all over the earth. Interestingly enough, the Mahdi will reign from Jerusalem, implying that the *Ka'ba,* the holy stone of Mecca, will also be transferred to that city.

According to Cook's research, the Egyptian writer Sa'id Ayyub emerged early as the leading contemporary advocate of Muslim apocalyptic thought. His book *The Antichrist* (1987)[16] has inspired other writers to come up with slightly different scenarios. Despite these variations, what they have in common is that the *dajjal* is a Jew, or Jewry in general, and his methods of control are conspiratorial. This *dajjal* has managed to take dominion over the United States of America and the European Community. Hence they view Israel's attempts to control Jerusalem and the Temple Mount with deep suspicion: it is the *dajjal* wishing to occupy the place of the Mahdi.

It is relatively easy to describe this kind of apocalyptic literature as an amalgam of traditional Muslim ideas, modern conspiracy theories, and burning anti-Semitism. It is not surprising, therefore, to see that Muslim end-time books and tracts are widely disseminated in Egypt and among the Palestinian people. It is also reasonable to assume that these writings have contributed to the Palestinian *intifadas;* and it is probable that they also influence suicide terrorists. The persistent anti-Semitism in them — the focus on the total destruction of Israel as the outcome of the yearned-for Apocalypse — is doubtless an important factor in the tensions of the Middle East.[17]

This brings me to the second reason why apocalyptic scenarios deserve our serious concern: it is their political usability — in other words, their political theology — that needs to be faced.

16. The title is Cook's translation of *Al-Masih al Dajjal* (Cairo: Faith li-l-A'lam al-'Arabi, 1987), a book that has not appeared in English translation.

17. The recently elected Iranian president, Mahmoud Ahmadinejad, has become notorious with his attacks on Israel. It now appears that he is profoundly influenced by apocalyptic scenarios within the Shiite branch of Islam, which awaits the return of the last legitimate imam, Abul Kassem Mohammed. He will reveal himself as the Mahdi, the end-time messiah who establishes the reign of justice on earth. Thus the disappearance of Israel becomes an end-time "necessity" (Rudolf Chimelli, "Der Mann, der aus der Tiefe kam," *Süddeutsche Zeitung* [Dec. 19, 2005], p. 3).

The Political Theology of Apocalyptic Scenarios

We are faced with Christian and Islamic apocalyptic scenarios that appeal to the same roots while they arrive at strictly opposite positions. They contain political messages that have already aggravated the conflict between Israel and the Palestinian people, and also between Israel and the Arab and Muslim peoples at large. The potential to ignite international conflicts even further is obvious.

The situation is even more dangerous because we also need to take into consideration the existence of a remarkably *strong apocalyptic movement within Judaism*. Gershom Gorenberg has described in detail how the aspirations of this Judaic movement center in the building of the Third Temple on the Temple Mount, which they consider the decisive apocalyptic requirement for the arrival of Messiah. Gorenberg also shows how apocalyptic Jewish groups cooperate with Christian apocalyptic communities in order to prepare for this end-time event. It goes without saying that the construction of the Third Temple would involve the destruction of the Muslim Dome of the Rock and/or the famous Al Aqsa Mosque — a scenario that would set the entire Muslim world on fire.[18]

Good versus Evil — A Dualistic Worldview

At first I thought it amusing that Tim LaHaye and Jerry Jenkins found their fictional Antichrist in Europe — in Romania, to be precise — and called him Nicolai Carpathia. For those who know a little about recent history, this Antichrist is clearly modeled after Nicolae Ceaușescu, the Romanian dictator who carried communism to its bloody extremes. "Carpathia" recalls the images of gruesome movie monsters such as Dracula and Frankenstein's beast. The political message is obvious: communism is the seedbed of the forces that produce the formidable "anti-Christ-coalition." Moreover, it is "old Europe," with its secular masses, that provides the context in which this Antichrist can

18. Gershom Gorenberg, *The End of Days: Fundamentalism and the Struggle for the Temple Mount* (Oxford and New York: Oxford University Press, 2002).

get started. And so it comes as no surprise that the *Left Behind* authors view the European Community as the base in which the Antichrist is consolidating his power.

Others will find it bizarre that the *dajjal* should be a Jew who rules the world from his home in Florida![19] But it would be careless to laugh off such fantastic imaginings. The implicit political message is suspicion and mistrust. How are Israelis and Palestinians ever going to agree on the issues that divide them if all practical political suggestions are seen in the light of sinister apocalyptic machinations? The implication of *Left Behind* is obvious: Be suspicious of the European powers. They may say that they are on the right side but, knowingly or not, they are doing the Antichrist's work.

This suspicion is further deepened when the authors of *Left Behind* "reveal" that Nicolai Carpathia has been the Secretary General of the United Nations before he discloses his true identity as the "Global Community's" potentate and ultimate enemy of Christ. This turns not only the European Community but also the United Nations into the platform for godless politics. Consequently, the true followers of Christ must be more than cautious of these organizations, to say the least: if they cannot be destroyed, they had better be carefully controlled in such a way that they become in fact powerless.

Once we know who the adversaries of Christ are, it is not difficult to find out where his followers can be found. In the narrative world of Tim LaHaye and Jerry Jenkins, the "messianic Christians" have their spiritual and strategic center at the "Strong Building" in Chicago. Most of them come from the "United North American States," and under the leadership of Rayford Matthews, a converted ex-pilot, the end-time warriors form the "Tribulation Force." They are aided by some Jews who have finally accepted Jesus as the Messiah.

It is clear to the authors of *Left Behind* that the true disciples of the coming Christ are mostly Americans. They are the messianic heroes, and they are on the right side, whereas the poor and misguided

---

19. This is the opinion of Muhammad 'Isa Da'ud in his book *Warning: the False Prophet is Invading the World from the Bermuda Triangle* (1992), quoted in David Cook, "Muslim Fears," p. 3 (the title of Da'ud's book is translated by Cook).

Europeans have chosen the wrong path and are bound to perish. There is very little that can be done about it because it is part of the final design of the Lord of history.

I investigate these Christian apocalyptic views in some detail because they concern me as a Christian in a more direct way than do the Islamic scenarios. But this is not to belittle the impact of Muslim apocalypticism. What the two have in common is their strict dualism, that is, they split the world up into the two opposite realms of good and evil. In doing so, they destroy the spaces peoples and nations require to tolerate each other, to arrive at sustainable relationships, and to share each other's values and riches. Furthermore, they imagine that the problems of the world are to be solved by totally dominating or even destroying those they identify as their enemies. David Cook's book-length study of contemporary Muslim apocalypticism gives evidence of their recurrent fantasy of setting the world right by destroying Israel, the United States, and the United Nations. And like the Christian apocalyptic thinkers, the Muslim scenario-makers are vague about how the world is to be ordered after evil is destroyed. The Mahdi will simply make it right.

For Christian observers, this dualism or dichotomy is reminiscent of the old heresy of Manichaeism. It is based on the teachings of the Persian Mani, who lived in the third century (216–c. 276 C.E.). Without going into details, suffice it to say that Mani taught a radical dualism. For him, the world was governed by two opposite divine powers, the God of Light and the God of Darkness, and history was marked by the attempts of Darkness to conquer the world. The human beings had elements of both "creators"; their ultimate calling was to purify themselves from their sins, or the shackles of darkness, by the strictest ascetic life possible. Only the Elected could hope to reach the Light. Mani's religion claimed to be the ultimate revelation and thus a synthesis of all prior religions. It spread widely — from Egypt to central China — and must have been a fierce competitor to the Christian communities in large parts of the Middle East.

The Christian Church (in particular St. Augustine, who was once an adherent of Manichaeism himself) has condemned this religious concept as heretical, mainly because it contradicts the Christian doc-

35

trine of a benevolent creation. For the early church, God is the only maker of all things and the sole ruler of history. While the early church did not deny the existence of the devil, or Satan, it was always certain that this "power of darkness" was ultimately subservient to the plans and powers of God. Nonetheless, Manichaeism remained a constant temptation, not as a competing organization but in the sense that its message seemed to confirm the everyday experience of people everywhere, namely, that they are immersed in an endless battle between good and evil. It remains seductive today because it reduces life's complexities to a much simpler either-or alternative.

And it is this reduction of the world's complexities that makes these apocalyptic scenarios attractive. Regardless of their numerous eccentric details, they offer a simplistic worldview that suggests straightforward political solutions where in fact there are none. Therefore, apocalyptic scenarios should not be dismissed as harmless. They contribute to a "spiritual climate" that enables people to simplify their grasp of the world. It permits them to find in the "satanic" or "evil" adversary a welcome focus for their sufferings and frustrations. So it provides them with a goal for their anger. If there are enough people adopting these views, and if they are active enough to promote them in their respective public and political realms, then such a climate might well gain a formative influence that politicians dare not ignore. It is sobering to learn from David Cook's survey that several Muslim scenarios, published long before 9/11, featured the destruction of New York City.[20]

For after all, these scenarios are seductive in their simplicity. Once you accept the premise that the world has reached its ultimate stage, what really matters is to be on the right side of the final showdown. That the others, including plants and animals, should be lost in the final annihilation is unavoidable. To quote Pat Robertson: "We are not to weep as the people of the world weep when there are certain tragedies or breakups of the government or systems of the world. . . . That isn't awful at all. It's good. It's a token, an evident token of our salvation. . . ."[21]

20. See Cook, *Contemporary Muslim Apocalyptic*, pp. 130, 163, 164-66.
21. Quoted by Tyler W. Stevenson, "Revelation's Warning to Evangelicals: *Left Behind* May Be Hazardous to Our Health" (*Reflections*, pp. 35f.).

It is this "us vs. them," "good vs. evil" dichotomy that is not only frightening when it is applied to personal relationships; it becomes downright threatening when it dominates political decision-making. For it sacrifices the search for sustainable solutions to the apparently clear-cut judgment of "whoever is not on my side is the enemy."

End Times Are War Times

Once the good-vs.-evil dichotomy has become acceptable in the realm of politics, there is little space left for the peaceful resolution of conflicts. On the contrary, the dichotomous worldview sees organizations that claim to work for world peace with suspicion because they may well be part of the ideological warfare launched by the Antichrist in order to confuse human beings about the true nature of the final confrontation. There can be no compromise between good and evil. In fact, the end of the world is needed in order to finally put an end to the evil powers. Hence everything in world history is heading toward a definitive confrontation. War becomes the necessary way in which God overcomes the forces of darkness. Tim LaHaye and Jerry Jenkins describe the horrors of their version of Armageddon with pornographic gusto: "Men and women, soldiers and horses seemed to explode where they stood. It was as if the very words of the Lord had superheated their blood, causing it to burst through the veins and skin."[22]

The same kind of violence can be found in Sa'id Ayyub: "Let the Christian know that he who lives by throwing bombs and with the policy of guns will meet tomorrow a Muslim whose patience has limits when his rights are taken. With blood! And with guns! . . . The land will be flowing with rainwater, but it will be red rainwater, sorry to say."[23]

22. Tim LaHaye and Jerry Jenkins, *Glorious Appearing*, vol. 12 of *Left Behind* (Wheaton, IL: Tyndale, 2004), quoted by Paul Boyer, "Give Me That End-Time Religion: The Politicization of Prophetic Belief in Contemporary America" (*Reflections*, p. 26).

23. S. Ayyub, *Aqidat al,masih al-Dajjal fi al-adyan* (Cairo: Dar al-Hadi, 1991), p. 195 (quoted by David Cook, "Muslim Fears," p. 3).

The political dimension is clear. The total embrace of violence has far-reaching implications for the ways people of the world address political conflicts. Surely, peace with justice cannot be a central component of end-time politics, nor can there be hope for the reconciliation of opponents and the healing of conflicts. On the contrary, the emphasis of end-time politics has to be on total confrontation. Disarmament cannot be the goal. Rather, in order to stay ahead of all possible threats, those who embrace confrontation will need to develop more and smarter arms — including nuclear weapons. This is the best justification the military-industrial complex could hope for!

The burden of threat, fear, and sorrow that we Europeans carry is the numerous times we have lived the history of hating enemies and destroying them. The carnage of those European wars was awful, but in some respects they look like "the good old days." We had the comparative luxury of destroying our armies and our cities before the time of massively destructive weapons. What will happen when apocalyptic minds, indifferent to the end of everything, are connected to the fingers that are on the nuclear trigger?

The Death of Creation

The embrace of violence not only leads to images of mass destruction of human beings; it willingly sacrifices the entire world, including the plants and animals. In the final battle, in the view of the apocalyptic believers, all of creation will be undone. Again, the political implications are far-reaching. Environmental concerns are not only fruitless (what can humans do against the will of God?); they are, in the final analysis, a sign of disbelief and disobedience to God's will. It is inevitable that there be extinctions of animal and plant species on an enormous scale. Likewise, there must be earthquakes and floods of unprecedented proportions. They are only some of the catastrophes that will accompany the "tribulations" that characterize the last days of humankind.

Bill Moyers, who received Harvard University's Global Environmental Citizen Award in 2004, refers to these thoughts in quoting

Glenn Scherer of the online journal *Grist,* who evokes apocalyptic attitudes in this way:

> Why care about the earth when the droughts, floods, famine and pestilence brought by ecological collapse are signs of the apocalypse foretold in the Bible? Why care about global climate change when you and yours will be rescued in the rapture? And why care about converting from oil to solar when the same God who performed the miracle of the loaves and fishes can whip up a few billion barrels of light crude with a word?[24]

Paradoxically, these apocalyptic scenarios do not pose any questions of accountability to the capitalist world order, of which the United States is the prime mover. Apparently, it does not bother the apocalyptic scenarists that Americans represent only 5 percent of the earth's population yet wastefully use up 25 percent of its oil and natural gas, to choose just one example of crucial resource use.[25] Why should it? If one takes the logic of the apocalypticists seriously, it is all up to God. Since God is all-powerful, he can provide as much as is needed — and much more. And if God gives you a good share of the riches of this world, then you should take them for granted as a token of divine blessing.

To quote Bill Moyers again:

> I . . . learned that the administration's friends at the International Policy Network, which is supported by Exxon Mobil and others of like mind, have issued a new report that climate change is "a myth, sea levels are not rising," [and] scientists who believe catastrophe is possible are "an embarrassment."[26]

24. Bill Moyers, "There is no tomorrow," *Minneapolis Star Tribune,* Jan. 30, 2005. Glenn Scherer's article was "The Godly Must Be Crazy," *Grist* (online), Oct. 27, 2004: http://www.grist.org/news/maindish/2004/10/27/scherer-christian/index.html (accessed Dec. 10, 2005).

25. See Rank Order charts for Oil Consumption, Natural Gas Consumption, and Population at the CIA Factbook (online): http://www.cia.gov/cia/publications/factbook (accessed Dec. 5, 2005).

26. Bill Moyers, "There is no tomorrow."

I am writing these words three days after Hurricane Katrina hit the southern coast of Mississippi, Alabama, and Louisiana, destroying many towns and drowning the city of New Orleans. I wonder how *Left Behind* readers in the nearby Bible belt will be reacting to this catastrophe. Will it shake their apocalyptic imagination about the "tribulations" of the last days, or will it reinforce their conviction that the end is indeed near?

Jerusalem: End-Time Capital

As noted above, the city of Jerusalem has a central place in the apocalyptic scenarios of Christian, Muslim, and Jewish end-time experts. This has a direct impact on the options of political leaders on all sides of the conflict. Nowhere else, it seems to me, does the "political theology" of end-time scenarios manifest itself so clearly and so threateningly. Jewish believers expect the messiah to reveal himself in the city of Jerusalem, convinced that he will enter the old walled-in city by opening the permanently closed Eastern Gate. Muslim apocalyptic authors affirm that the Mahdi will rule the world from that same site. For Christian authors such as Tim LaHaye and others, Jerusalem must be fully in the hands of the Jewish people before Jesus can return. The Third Temple must be built on the Temple Mount, which implies that the Al Aqsa Mosque and the Dome of Rock must be removed — either by divine intervention or by some less mysterious earthly weapon. There is no need to make detailed reference to the conservative Christian groups in the United States, the Netherlands, and other countries that actively support Jews who want to return to the Holy Land, who are backing Jewish settlements in the occupied Palestinian territories, who are involved in getting the Third Temple started, and so forth.[27]

Pat Robertson has said, "The Bible Belt is Israel's safety net in the U.S.A.," a statement I consider to be plainly — though unintentionally perhaps — cynical. He and other end-time specialists admit that the

---

27. See Gorenberg, *The End of Days*, pp. 7-29, for a detailed description of the search for the red heifer that is needed for the sacrifices at the Third Temple.

gathering of the Jews in their Promised Land is nothing but a precondition for the Second Coming of Christ. They are counting on 144,000 Jews to accept Jesus as their messiah; the rest belong to the *massa perditionis* — the condemned masses. When the real Messiah comes, the land of Israel will be turned into the final battlefield, where all the armies of the earth will converge. This, then, is the "final solution": the state of Israel will disappear. This implies that all Jews who have not accepted Christ will also be annihilated. What kind of "safety net" is that? I believe that such a genocidal imagination displays a shocking lust for violence. At the center of such faith lies practical nihilism. Yehezkel Landau, a dual Israeli-American citizen and peace educator, aptly comments:

> With family and friends in and around Jerusalem, I shudder to think of what might happen to those I love and to all the inhabitants of the Holy Land if the end-time program of these Christian dualists ever materializes. Sadly the danger is compounded by an unholy alliance they have made with Jewish apocalypticists whose pseudo-messianic dream focuses on a third Jewish temple replacing the Dome of the Rock and Al-Aqsa-Mosque. The end-times dream of these fanatical Jews and Christians is, in reality, a nightmare for everyone else, since it would entail an all-out Jewish/Christian war with the Muslim world.[28]

As a German citizen, I feel very strongly about this: the heaviest burden that we Germans have to carry is the Holocaust, the near extinction of European Jewry by Hitler's "willing executioners." Therefore, I am deeply committed to the safety of the Israeli state. This implies that I want the state of Israel to become a permanent part of the Middle East, a state in which Jews of various backgrounds and commitments can live together without fear of pogroms and genocidal threats. This implies, furthermore, that Israeli governments will work

28. Jehezkel Landau, in his review article of Barbara R. Rossing's *The Rapture Exposed: The Message of Hope in the Book of Revelation* (Boulder, CO: Westview Press, 2004), in *Conversations in Religion and Theology* (Hartford Seminary) 3, no. 1 (May 2000): 54-60.

on building just and sustainable relationships with their neighbors, especially with the Palestinians, who have justifiable claims to the same lands and to the city of Jerusalem.

Therefore, the worst thing that Christians can envision for Israel is to inflame her already problematic relationships with her neighbors by turning the Holy Land into an apocalyptic battlefield. I believe that it will also be in Israel's best interests for the European countries and the United States to assist the neighboring Arab nations in working toward just and democratically sustainable situations, and to help a Palestinian state begin functioning within clear borders. The future of Israel cannot be sustained in a constant warfare with the neighboring peoples and by further shaming and humiliating them. It is probable that these experiences of impotence have contributed to the rapid growth of Muslim apocalypticism. Thus, we need to do everything in our power to reconstruct a sense of dignity in the Arab peoples, to neutralize their self-destructive fury, and to create space for the establishment of fair relationships.

No Need to Think Twice

There is another element that comes into play if one reflects on the impact of apocalyptic end-time scenarios. Since God, in his supreme wisdom, has ordained that world history must run its confrontational course, the obedient response of faithful followers is to consider themselves nothing more than instruments of God's design. God is the real subject and thus ultimately responsible; the accountability of believers lies in their obedience to God. This, in turn, relieves them of a direct responsibility to deal with life's various problems. Once they have accepted the providential either-or framework of history, they can view the complexities of their personal existence and the challenges of their professional work either as a confirmation of faith or as a test of faith. In neither case is it necessary to worry too much about the intellectual challenges or the ethical problems, because it is the servant's duty to obey, and not to doubt, the ways of God. Obviously, getting rid of responsibility is a tremendous relief, especially to women and men who are overburdened by the complexities and ambiguities of modern daily life. They are relieved of seeking complicated compromises to complex issues. The scientific and moral challenges can be reduced, because God himself has made them exceptionally clear. What God demands is obedience, pure and simple.

Such a perspective is especially tempting to people in leadership positions; for if obedience is the decisive thing, they need not worry about the guilt that is part and parcel of their high offices. I am not referring to errors: they are part of our human predicament and can be explained and corrected, though it may at times involve great cost. I am referring to guilt as an inevitable consequence of conscious decision-making. Every decision for one option implies decisions that exclude others; every choice of one person means the rejection of others who are equally qualified. It is thus naive to assume that people in power can get around the reality of guilt. Guilt is the shadow of power. If people in power can delegate their power — and its consequences — to the supreme Lord of history, they need not face the painful weight of guilt. The tremendous relief that an apocalyptic either-or faith provides is that, if one is a good servant in the eyes of the Creator, one can never be ultimately wrong, regardless of what others say.

The Apocalyptic Trap

Earlier I raised the question of whether a preoccupation with end-time scenarios is "indigenous" to American religious culture. As my references to Muslim apocalyptic writings illustrate, it is obviously wrong to say that the "doom-boom" industry is an exclusively American affair. We can say, however, that apocalyptic scenarios abound where there are strong messianic — and, more specifically, millennialist — traditions. I do not wish to overemphasize the similarities between Muslim and Christian apocalypticism. But it is possible to note that, in both versions, the apocalyptic scenarios are based on specific eschatological traditions. Whenever eschatological expectations are framed into absolutized end-time scenarios, they end up in a trap: end-time scenarios are dead ends because they pretend to be the only and ultimate consequence of a millennialist reading of history. In this sense they are caricatures of genuine messianic hopes.

In the case of Islam, one cannot deny that it possesses strong eschatological components inasmuch as it considers itself to be the final manifestation of God's will, revealed by the prophet Muhammad, and thus called to provide the "right order" for the entire world. This claim appeared to be gloriously confirmed in the rapid expansion of Islam during the seventh and eighth centuries C.E. Islam had established itself as the world's "superpower," stretching from India in the east to Spain in the west. One cannot deny that the Muslim Empire was the most modern and tolerant realm during the Middle Ages. The Christian societies of Europe profited from it more than they wish to admit today. Therefore, there are many favorable things one can and must say about the early Muslim empires, and it is understandable that Muslims today are very proud of this part of their past.

However, it is a misguided pride. Taking up Vamik Volkan's term, we might say that the early Muslim Empire became the "chosen triumph" of the Arabic people. It was turned into the key by which they could interpret their global destiny. Even terrorist groups such as Al Qaeda use this chosen triumph hermeneutics to justify their murderous attacks. They murder "infidels" and "apostates" in order to usher in the final reign of their God. At the same time, this kind of hermeneutic makes it easy for Muslims to place the blame for the slow decline of Muslim empires — including their present impotence — exclusively on the destructive invasions, the "crusades," of the Western powers. Compared to the early greatness of Muslim empires, they feel their steady decline into powerlessness as a terrible humiliation. But since they dare not attribute this shame to Allah (which would cause a deep religious crisis), nor to the self-destructive impact of corruption and divisions within the Islamic world (which would sharpen internal social and political crises), they must place the blame on the "satanic" powers of the Jews or other "infidels," of whom those in the United States are the latest and most powerful manifestation.

It is deplorable, though hardly surprising, that Muslim apocalypticism has assumed a more murderous intensity today than it has ever had before. It mirrors Christian apocalypticism, which has gained unprecedented influence in the United States. Indeed, David Cook's survey shows that contemporary Muslim apocalypse-scenario writers have read Christian authors such as Billy Graham, Jerry Falwell, and Pat Robertson — sometimes quoting them as authorities![29] And we can safely assume that both sides would tend to overestimate the power of the adversary. But that does not make the matter less dangerous. According to the characteristics outlined above, the apocalyptic theology of the *Left Behind*–influenced believers leads the Christian faith into a dead-end situation. It turns its own interpretation of the Bible into absolute truth and thus leaves no room for any debate about the internal variety within Holy Scripture and the various foci of the Christian faith. It sets history on a confrontational course toward final annihilation that allows no alternatives to surface. Furthermore, it turns believers into faithful instruments of God's supreme action and thus robs them of personal responsibility. In other words, it is a faith without compassion for one's own community, a faith without personal accountability (except for "personal," i.e., mostly sexual, sins). Come to think of it, it is a faith filled with despair and denial. This explains the images in *Left Behind* of genocidal violence and annihilating fury.

End-Time Games in an End-Time World

It has often been said that 9/11 was a turning point in history. But there are also the "end-time experts" who claim that 1948 (the founding of the state of Israel) was a decisive turning point. It would be more accurate, however, to say that world history took an unprecedented turn on August 6, 1945. With the first dropping of atomic bombs on two Japanese cities, the world entered the stage in which a total destruction of life on this planet is possible at any time. The decision to use two atomic bombs came at the end of World War II, which was a historical moment wrought with murderous excesses the likes of which the world had never seen before. Tens of millions had been killed, many

29. Cook, *Contemporary Muslim Apocalyptic*, p. 92.

millions were made refugees, and entire cities lay in ruins. To bring this carnage to an end — by whatever means — was something the world longed for. And to punish those nations who had started it — by whatever means — may have seemed to many a matter of gruesome justice.

Out of this avalanche of hatred and fury the real end-time was born, and now humankind must live with it. In the words of Jürgen Moltmann:

> Hiroshima 1945 fundamentally changed the quality of human history: *our time has become time with a time-limit.* . . . This time of ours, when humanity can be brought to an end at any moment, is indeed, in a purely secular sense and without any apocalyptic images, the "end-time"; for no one can expect that this nuclear era will be succeeded by another in which humanity's deadly threat to itself will cease to exist.[30]

Sixty years later, there are arsenals of nuclear weaponry that can kill all living things many times over. In everyday life we do all we can to deny this reality. But the nervousness with which the atomic powers attempt to prevent others from joining "the club" — as I write this, Iran is the latest case in point — indicates that governments do know how threatening this annihilating scenario is. All the rest of us go on with our lives as if this ultimate danger did not exist. We pay for the "normality" of life with massive denial. For how are we to exist with the constant awareness of this mortal threat? Denial is a way to avoid feelings of futility and uselessness. Even peace activists who attempt to struggle for nuclear disarmament cannot avoid the paralysis of denial, because the fact is evident that, even if they were successful, the end-time reality would continue to exist. The "bomb" has been invented, and the knowledge of how to construct it is available around the world. Even if all existing nuclear devices could be destroyed today, the formula to construct them anew is at hand. We all have to live with this fact. To be conscious of this ultimate power of destruction and to organize the affairs of the world's nations in such a way as to avoid its use, therefore,

---

30. Moltmann, *Coming of God*, pp. 205-6 (italics in original).

has become the supreme responsibility of all political leaders. For the last sixty years our political establishments have kept this frightful task in mind, though there have been situations in which the world was on the brink of nuclear warfare anyway. Henceforth, this vigilance needs to be sustained and cultivated in all coming generations.

In 1945 it was only the nuclear hell that had to be accounted for. During more recent decades human-made environmental disasters have increased to a degree that large parts of the earth may become permanently uninhabitable.[31] Hurricanes Katrina and Rita have shown that low-lying coastal areas can no longer be inhabited in the same careless way they were before. One need not be a prophet to see that our customary ways of living will come under increasing pressure. If the peoples of the world are to continue existing under fairly acceptable conditions, all of them need to accept our general end-time reality. It is a reality brought about by human beings, and it is to be accounted for by human beings.

What is the relationship between this end-time situation and the stupendous growth of religious end-time scenarios, especially in the United States? One could plausibly answer that, up until now, the United States has been the only power to have used nuclear bombs. Furthermore, the production of more and more sophisticated nuclear weapons has increased to a degree that their destructive violence is beyond imagination. But what can be done about this awesome reality and the confusing feelings of guilt, despair, and hopelessness that it generates? Everything appears to have gotten out of control.

We reach a psychological impasse here, to which apocalyptic end-time scenarios seem to present a "liberating" response. Since they tell us that the world is full of evil powers, the presence of nuclear weapons begins to make sense. Because world history is headed toward a final all-consuming war, the annihilating powers of nuclear weapons can be seen as inevitable — or even desirable. Thus it makes sense to assume that nuclear weapons are part of the "tribulations" of the last

31. See Climate Change Report 2001: Synthesis Report, Summary for Policymakers, An Assessment of the Intergovernmental Panel on Climate Change, approved in detail at IPCC Plenary XVIII (Wembley, United Kingdom, Sept. 24-29, 2001).

days. This "faith" replaces responsibility, shifting the final accountability for these weapons of mass destruction to a metaphysical level. In the end, the nuclear threat is part of God's design.

This is a psychological mechanism that turns despair into "faith." Furthermore, it provides an outlet for repressed guilt and helplessness: the hidden angst is transformed into the "righteous anger," which justifies the genocidal images of end-time horrors and wars. The pornographic violence that manifests itself in the imagery of *Glorious Appearing,* the twelfth volume of *Left Behind,* is a perfect example of how despairing feelings of impotence can be transformed into images of divinely sanctioned, murderous omnipotence: the only way to "save" the world is to destroy it.

I believe that this may be a possible explanation for the stupendous success of end-time religious fiction such as *Left Behind.* It would also enable us to perceive the amount of profound despair, rather than joyful faith, that lies at the heart of this end-time religion. But if this is correct, it raises questions about the corruptibility of messianism itself.

CHAPTER 3

Winner Takes Too Much

———⟨ɷⱵ⟩———

Long before I came to America, America came to me. I was five years old when I saw my first Americans. They were GI's who in the spring of 1945 rushed up in their car to my parents' farm. They did not stay long. What they were looking for I do not know. My younger brother and I just stood there staring at them in their impressive outfits. The Americans came to us as the liberators, the winners par excellence. Some people of my parents' generation eyed them with resentment. But many among them — the "Amis," as they were called — greeted the Americans with immense relief. Furthermore, the CARE packages arrived in our hunger-stricken country beginning in February 1946, and they sustained millions of desperate people. This vital relief created a profound gratitude toward the United States, which has never been forgotten by Germans. The life-saving importance of the CARE packages is illustrated by the following example. A young woman published an offer of marriage in a newspaper with the following text: "Offered: A two-room apartment and two CARE packages per month." She received 2,437 responses from freezing and hungry men![1]

1. Godehard Weyerer, "C.A.R.E. für Deutschland," *Die Zeit* (July 24, 1996).

49

For us, the post–World War II children and young people, everything American was better and more attractive than what we had before. The "American way of life" was the model of a bright life we could have. We were the losers, and Germany lay in ruins. All our fantasies of the good life focused on stories of the proverbial American self-made man who had started as a dishwasher, only to become the wealthy owner of factories, banks, and ships.

Later on, in high school, we were introduced to American writers — literature such as Hemingway's short stories, Thomas Wolfe's *Look Homeward, Angel,* and plays by Eugene O'Neill and Tennessee Williams. Our teachers, many of them old enough to have experienced the self-immunizing ideology of the Hitler years, took relish in discovering the literature, architecture, and arts of our liberators. (We discovered their music for ourselves!) This fascination doubtless influenced my decision to travel to the United States for further studies. In the early 1960s it was simply obvious that you would go there if you wanted to get on in life.

I say this without irony: the American way of life was the role model that attracted the Germans of my generation. It was, if I may say so, our guiding myth because it combined greatness and generosity, strength and competence — and a lot of fun. Its democratic traditions and its advocacy for peace with freedom was hugely more attractive to us than the grim reality of the nearby socialist countries dominated by the Soviet Union. When President John F. Kennedy came to Berlin in 1962, he was enthusiastically welcomed by huge crowds. "Ich bin ein Berliner," the president said. The Berliners would have loved to respond by saying, *Wir sind alle Amerikaner!* ("We are all Americans!").

To be sure, there was a good bit of naiveté in this image of America. Its appeal was largely shaped and enhanced by the Hollywood movies, which brought to us the stories of the typical American hero, who always came out the victor over any foe who stood in his way — many of them, of course, sinister Nazis. He was the perfect winner, nonchalantly shrugging off the admiration of those he had saved, while his irresistible charm won him the attention of the most dazzling women.

It has sometimes been said that Germany is the most Americanized country in Europe. My explanation would be that Germany came out of World War II as a nation utterly defeated, not only in material terms but, even more perhaps, in spiritual and moral ways. Since there seemed to be nothing left in our history worthy for us to rely on for the reconstruction of our identity, we looked to our victors for a meaningful substitute. It has taken some decades for us to reappropriate the great things of German history, the legacies of our important poets and composers, theologians and philosophers, artists and scientists — while at the same time remembering the atrocities of the Third Reich. It was, and is, difficult for us to love our country deeply enough to remember that it produced both Goethe and Goebbels, both Weimar and Buchenwald. In fact, this struggle to simultaneously hold in our minds both the evil aspects and the beautiful aspects of our history will continue — and must continue. It is a sobering consciousness of identity that can lead to the recognition that all human beings and all nations need to work for an integrated awareness of their positive and negative qualities: it is a more mature national identity that places both "winner" and "loser" aspects in the foreground.

The Winner-Loser Syndrome

It has just so happened that I have lived outside Germany for many years. Perhaps more than others who have stayed closer to home, I was compelled to answer troubling questions about what it means to be German. This has helped me to arrive at a sense of identity as a German citizen, an identity that encompasses the complex legacies of guilt and glory, shame and pride. This process was painful, but it has led me to work on a critical appraisal of a cultural phenomenon that is in many ways related to the so-called American way of life: I call it the "winner-loser syndrome." "Winner takes all" is more than the title of a song or a rule in electoral procedures.[2] In the American way of

2. The song "Winner Takes All" was recorded by Abba in 1980. Concerning elections, in contrast to the voting rights in Great Britain and the United States, where the

life, it has become a subtle way to classify human beings and to divide society.

What I have in mind can be illustrated by a story a friend told me some time ago. One of his sons was a member of the high school football team in their hometown, and though the team represented a small school, it had made it all the way to the deciding game of the state championship. But they lost that championship game; the other team became Number One. Even so, as any mature person would have felt, they had, against all odds, managed to be the second best team in the state. But this apparently did not count with their coach. When the players got back to their locker room, the coach went berserk: "You are losers," he yelled. "You are goddamned losers!" On and on he ranted with the cruel verdict.

My issue here is not to analyze the cruel and immature behavior of a coach degrading the achievement of his own players. My concern is rather with the kind of categorical, ontological judgment that his behavior exemplifies. Don't misunderstand me. I am all for excellence. In my opinion, there is nothing wrong with people who try to do their best, and high schools and universities should encourage their students to work for the best possible results, whether in scholarly or athletic pursuits. To do something meaningful is essential for human existence on this earth. No child should be denied the experience of discovering his or her gifts and putting them to good use. But it is precisely because I wish to see as many people as possible grow into their fullness that I am critical of the winner-loser syndrome. Essentially, it contains the philosophical error of turning *incidents* (i.e., losing a game, winning a deal, etc.) into a permanent anthropological *state*. The error is considering things that are merely *happening* to human beings to be part of their *being* — even *to constitute their being*.

---

winning candidate takes all the votes of a constituency while those for his/her opponents are simply lost, German citizens have two separate votes. One goes directly to a candidate, the other to a political party. This system enables smaller parties such as the Greens or the Liberals to send members to the Parliament who have been elected via the party vote. I prefer this system to the British or American systems, which create almost insuperable burdens for fresh political ideas and parties to enter into the parliamentary processes.

But it is more than a philosophical error. To be classified a winner or a loser implies a judgment with far-reaching social and political consequences. With this in mind, let's take a look at what the winner-loser syndrome does to the "losers." It is common knowledge that the lack of appreciation starves children of their potential. Yet it is also a commonplace experience that parents and teachers and peers often label children losers if the children don't live up to their expectations. This verdict goes hand in hand with a loss of love, admiration, and joy. It happens in homes and schools around the world: we see children trying to do their best, yet without success, while others are brighter, faster, or more beautiful. To grow up with the experience that it is always the others who have better grades, richer parents, fancier clothes, and happier smiles makes children insecure about themselves. The "loser" verdict incapacitates them.

Along with this comes *shaming,* a terrible reality in the lives of the losers. Shaming destroys persons from within: it forces them to live, as it were, with a deflated sense of self. This applies not only to children and young people; it also applies to adults in their marital or professional lives. It would be far too simple to suggest that people on the losing side in life should simply "demythologize" the erroneous character of the winner-loser syndrome and thus liberate themselves from it. Far from it. Once one has internalized the "loser" verdict, it becomes extremely difficult to overcome it in constructive ways. For that would require a kind of sovereignty over self that most "losers" cannot attain. In fact, the tragedy is that the models by which they assess themselves have been set by the mighty and the powerful, the rich and the beautiful, the strong and the successful — those who determine the images of what a "real" human being should be.

How are people supposed to get on with their lives when they are constantly confronted with signals that tell them, "You are a failure! A nobody! A goddamned loser!"? Living with self-contempt, bitterness, and envy is not healthy. Few persons will find the energy to face their feeling of total defeat. Fortunately, there are self-help groups, such as Alcoholics Anonymous and other "anonymous" gatherings, that enable people to share their devastating experiences with others who are facing the same ordeals. They provide a communal space where positive energies can be created out of negative feelings. But not many people find this way out. They likely think that self-help groups such as A.A. are only for people who are really lost in a form of deep addiction. Rather, most "losers" will be tempted to seek situations in which they appear to be "winners." One way of acting out this urge is through violence: "losers" will lord it over people who are close to them, because it is always possible to find smaller and weaker persons — for example, women or children. The resulting so-called horizontal violence can be seen in the battering of wives and children.[3]

A common way out is to compensate for the deflated sense of self by joining a secret society or a gang, thus participating in the enlarged self of a group. The camaraderie-complicity of the group provides the illusion of belonging to a larger self that is a "winner." The violent attacks of such groups provide instant satisfaction, based on their heroic illusion. This impression of being a winner needs to be re-created, thus accounting for the urge of such groups to repeat their violent behavior. The consequences are there for all to see: the ego of the gang affirms itself in the violence they use to crush weaker groups. Gangs can cloak their violence by constructing a "mission," which gives them the right to punish others for their allegedly inferior — or "infidel" — state. The pattern requires that, to set oneself up as a winner, one has to create losers. This mechanism inevitably creates the downward spiral of violence and keeps it in motion.

We should also briefly look at a related question: *What does the winner-loser syndrome do to the "winners"?* Children who have grown up with the experience of being on top will learn to assume that this is the normal state of things. Once they get into situations of severe competition, for instance, in college or in the work place, they will have to become fiercely competitive in order to stay on top. To remain a winner means to be prepared to sacrifice oneself and others. To be on top implies that one is standing on a pyramid of contenders who did not make it. So there is considerable symbolic violence involved in

---

3. The violent character of the winner-loser syndrome I discuss at greater detail in my essay in Geiko Müller-Fahrenholz, ed., *Faszination Gewalt. Aufklärungsversuche* (Frankfurt/Main: Lembeck Verlag, 2006), pp. 66-98.

asserting oneself as a winner. Incidentally, as one studies the success stories of "born winners," one is struck by how often a spouse or one of the children takes upon herself or himself the dark side of the hero. This is the proverbial black sheep in "number one" families.

It is part of the violence implied in the winner posture that one must deny the responsibility for the costs and sacrifices. One cannot entertain questions about inequalities, injustices, or abuses of power. The winners take it all, and they deserve it all — a fatal ethical consequence. The illusion is that it is all their own doing, as if they had created themselves out of nothing. Hence they are not responsible for the ones they shove aside, or the manner in which they do it, unless it is grossly illegal. Those who have not "made it" have only themselves to blame; it's their own guilt if they have failed. It is part of the winner posture to ensure that this kind of thinking is socially acceptable. This is relatively easy because part of their power lies in the authority to create the models and images by which society regards itself. Hence the winner-loser syndrome appears as the "normal" state of things.

These brief psycho-social reflections lead to a further question: *What does the winner-loser syndrome do to society?* Obviously, it has an impact on how one understands and conducts relationships with political opponents, neighboring peoples, or ethnic groups. Although its rationale purports to do nothing more than seek excellence, and although it is inevitable that some should be more successful than others, the winner-loser syndrome introduces an element of division that dissolves the essential connectedness and mutuality between its members that every community depends on. If we allow distinctions between "winners" and "losers" to attain a quasi-ontological status, we introduce a dichotomy that is apt to destroy the humanness that is common to all human beings regardless of their performances and failures.

When Hurricane Katrina hit New Orleans, television reports clearly showed that its poorest residents had suffered the most. Many viewers in the United States and beyond were appalled by the fact that many of these residents of the "Big Easy" had been left behind on rooftops and in neglected shelter locations. Of the host of angry commentators, I will quote only two. Bob Herbert, of the *New York*

Times, spoke of the "dangerous incompetence and the staggering indifference to human suffering of the president and his administration."[4] His fellow columnist, Thomas L. Friedman, a fervent supporter of President Bush's reaction to 9/11, wrote:

> So many of the things the Bush team has ignored or distorted under the guise of fighting Osama were exposed by Katrina: its refusal to impose a gasoline tax after 9/11, which would have begun to shift our economy much sooner to more fuel-efficient cars, helped raise money for a rainy day and eased our dependence on the world's worst regimes for energy; its refusal to develop some form of national health care to cover the 40 million uninsured.[5]

Are these reactions an indicator that the United States will be going in the direction of establishing what Europeans consider vital aspects of the welfare state system? Some doubts are in order. Jedediah Purdy, a professor of law at Duke University, points out that most Americans — roughly 90 percent, including African-Americans — consider the United States a just society.[6] The rules of social and economic life are fair, they have said in polls. Effort is being honored, and all human beings get their chance. It is striking that 20 percent thought that they belonged to the richest 1 percent of American society, and another 20 percent thought that they would soon belong to that privileged group. Purdy continues:

> The flip side of this optimism is the suspicion that, if you end up poor or sick or alone, the fault must be in you, and the judgment belongs on you. It is the American habit to admire the rich and powerful and recoil from the weak and poor — even if the weak and poor include one's self. The result is a political culture

4. Bob Herbert, "Bush's Colossal Failure," *New York Times,* Sept. 5, 2005.

5. Thomas L. Friedman, "Osama and Katrina," *New York Times,* Sept. 7, 2005.

6. Jedediah Purdy, "Eine Lehrstunde für Wölfe," *Süddeutsche Zeitung* 37 (Sept. 8, 2005), p. 3. (The quote is taken from the unpublished English original, which J. Purdy has kindly permitted me to use.)

where policies meant to aid the disadvantaged — such as welfare payments, universal health care, and racial preferences in hiring — are regarded as intrusions on the natural order.

If Purdy's analysis of Americans' way of thinking is correct, it is a clear expression of the winner-loser syndrome. If this is what a majority of U.S. citizens feels about how a good society should be organized, one cannot expect much admiration for the European state welfare systems. Obviously, this does not mean that there should be no solidarity with the weak and poor at all. This becomes a matter of generosity, and religious or humanistic institutions are called to respond (they have done so in the United States in great measure) — but not the state. By contrast, most Europeans consider it a fundamental duty of the state to work for social justice, while at the same time affirming that additional forms of solidarity are indispensable.

A political culture that is structured along the winner-loser divide has far-reaching implications for international relations. International conflicts would leave little room for negotiations: any compromise would make the winner look like a coward. Thus an either-or stalemate is bound to dominate relationships. Needless to say, once entire nations are considered "losers," the expression "failed state" becomes quite revealing. The "failed" are placed in situations of collective shame. The way they are treated, for instance, by the International Monetary Fund or the World Bank often intensifies the feeling that they have been robbed of their dignity. But it is evident that self-respect is the ultimate precondition for a nation to recover and to enter into meaningful cooperation with others. It is virtually impossible to arrive at mutual confidence when relationships are seen through the lens of the winner-loser dichotomy; on the contrary, it is bound to sharpen polarizations and warfare. The "war on terrorism" is a clear example. The Bush administration introduced it as the only way to deal with international terrorism; consequently, they labeled the efforts by other countries to arrive at more nuanced and comprehensive responses to confront terrorist attacks as policies of cowardly "appeasement."[7]

7. A clear example of this either-or approach can be seen in David Frum and Richard

The Myth of the American Superhero

The winner-loser syndrome is a psycho-social way to understand an important strand in the American way of life — which, needless to say, has spread to most parts of the world. This approach is closely related to the analysis of American popular culture that Robert Jewett and John Lawrence have presented in their two books, *The Myth of the American Superhero* and *Captain America and the Crusade Against Evil: The Dilemma of Zealous Nationalism*.[8] They have shown, convincingly I believe, that American popular culture during the twentieth century has been in the thrall of the mythical figure of the lone hero who singlehandedly redeems a community in distress. According to Jewett and Lawrence, the "archetypal plot formula" that "may be seen in thousands of popular-culture artifacts" is:

> A community in a harmonious paradise is threatened by evil; normal institutions fail to contend with the threat; a selfless superhero emerges to renounce temptations and carry out the redemptive task; aided by fate, his decisive victory restores the community to its paradisiacal condition; the superhero then recedes into obscurity.[9]

The two authors insist that this American monomyth is different from the classical monomyth that Joseph Campbell has aptly described in *The Hero with a Thousand Faces*.[10] Whereas the classical hero ven-

Perle, *An End to Evil: How to Win the War on Terror* (New York: Random House, 2003). The authors state: "We do not believe that Americans are fighting this evil [i.e., of terrorism] to minimize it or to manage it. We believe they are fighting to win — to end this evil before it kills again and on a genocidal scale. There is no middle way for Americans: It is victory or holocaust" (p. 9), a listing of options that I as a German find terrifying.

8. John Shelton Lawrence and Robert Jewett, *The Myth of the American Superhero* (Grand Rapids: Eerdmans, 2002); Robert Jewett and John Shelton Lawrence, *Captain America and the Crusade Against Evil: The Dilemma of Zealous Nationalism* (Grand Rapids: Eerdmans, 2003).

9. Lawrence and Jewett, *Myth*, p. 6.

10. Joseph Campbell, *The Hero with a Thousand Faces* (New York: Meridian, 1956).

tures out as a youth into a world of wonder and danger and learns to overcome threatening adversaries in order to return home a more mature and wiser human being, the American superhero is both the selfless servant who risks his life for others and the "zealous crusader who destroys evil."[11] While the classical hero seems derived from initiation rites aimed at the maturation of ordinary individuals, the American hero reflects the imagery of redemption. In the words of Jewett and Lawrence:

> The supersaviors in pop culture function as replacements for the Christ figure, whose credibility was eroded by scientific rationalism. But their superhuman abilities reflect a hope for divine, redemptive powers that science has never eradicated from the popular mind. Figures such as Neo in *The Matrix* seem explicitly designed to offer contemporary moviegoers this new Christ — one who has dropped the ineffectual baggage of the Sermon on the Mount. Instead, he and his shooting partner Trinity carry a duffel bag full of pistols, guns, and explosives needed to destroy the command center of political evil.[12]

We need not enumerate the various explanations and illustrations with which Jewett and Lawrence substantiate their point. But they show that the fantasies range all the way from the lone cowboy or sheriff in classic western movies such as *High Noon* to presidents whose superheroic powers save the entire world (as in *Independence Day* and *Air Force One*). But the superhero is not only found in movies; he dominates television series and video games. The authors give special attention to the *Star Trek* television series and the *Star Wars* movie series because in them they discover a fascination with violence bordering on pop fascism:

> We are hardly suggesting that George Lucas is a European fascist or that the millions of Americans who flocked to *Star Wars*

11. Lawrence and Jewett, *Myth*, p. 6.
12. Lawrence and Jewett, *Myth*, pp. 6f.

and its sequels are a new wave of Brown Shirts or *Hitlerjugend*. Instead, there is an indigenous American tradition of violent redemption that surfaces in this film, an undercurrent that runs parallel to European streams of idealistic crusading. . . . Furthermore, the notion that all of life resolves into clear-cut battles between good and evil is itself antithetical to the democratic understanding of governance. . . . Showing the spiritual affinities of *Star Wars* with fascism suggests the profoundly antidemocratic spirit of this stream that continues to flow through the American imagination.[13]

I would like to make two observations. First, it is understandable that Jewett and Lawrence should be concerned with the impact of superheroic fantasies on the democratic institutions of their nation, concerned that these fantasies can shape the popular culture of the United States to a degree that could threaten the vitality and resilience of its democratic institutions. In a way, their analysis sharpens the dichotomy I have described in the winner-loser syndrome. While the hero is the winner par excellence, the endangered communities they come to save, those waiting for a savior because they cannot redeem themselves, are the losers. In other words, democratic institutions are on the losing edge and always in need of the superhuman hero who will win their battles for them. Whether or not these authors' analysis appropriately describes the political situation in the United States, I am not in a position to judge.

My second observation — something that concerns me greatly — is that the pop fascism we are dealing with is by no means a purely American affair. Superhero fantasies have made their way around the world and have found a place in the imagination of millions of human beings in the far corners of the earth. Not only have Coca Cola, McDonald's, and Microsoft conquered the world; the same holds true, because of the global proliferation of American television and cinema, for the more subversive fascination with a superhuman hero who promises to do the heavy lifting for all those who are too weak to help themselves. It may

13. Lawrence and Jewett, *Myth*, p. 278.

well be that this way of elevating the winner-loser divide to quasi-mythological heights is steadily contaminating the beliefs of people in the efficacy of their own democratic institutions, not only in the United States but everywhere. This is a trend at odds with the official political goal of establishing viable democracies around the world.

Lawrence and Jewett are speaking of "paradoxes" here.[14] For many observers from outside, however — especially those who are already skeptical of Western-style democracies — the winner-superhero imagery may well make them even more suspicious. Especially in those cases in which political leaders are setting themselves up as superheroes, the message is ambivalent, to say the least. What I have in mind is well illustrated by the following incident.

The February 12, 2002, edition of the German weekly magazine *Der Spiegel* had a cover-collage that gave me a start when I took it out of my mailbox. In order to illustrate the crusade-like fight of the Bush administration against international terrorism — and Saddam Hussein in particular — *Der Spiegel's* satirical cover portrayed President Bush as Rambo holding an automatic gun in his arms and ammunition belts around his muscular body; Vice President Cheney was "the Terminator"; (former) National Security Adviser Condoleezza Rice came out as Xena, Warrior Princess; Secretary of State Colin Powell was presented as Batman; and Secretary of Defense Donald Rumsfeld was Conan the Barbarian. The cover collage was meant to be a satirical set-up for the lead article inside the magazine, and I felt that it was a *lèse majesté*, so to speak — an insult to the high office of the president of the United States. But, to my surprise, it was not received by the targets of the satire that way at all! The then U.S. Ambassador to Germany, Daniel Coats, visited the offices of *Der Spiegel,* not to protest, but to say that President Bush was "flattered." Coats then ordered thirty-three copies of the cover to be enlarged to poster size and sent to the White House because each member of Bush's staff reportedly wanted one.[15]

It is difficult to say whether this is anything more than a funny episode. But it does illustrate that the superhero fantasies are playfully ac-

---

14. See Lawrence and Jewett, *Myth*, p. 7.
15. For more details, see Jewett and Lawrence, *Captain America*, pp. 40, 43.

cepted at the highest offices of power. It is not only "pop fascism," however, that concerns Jewett and Lawrence. They are equally worried about the contempt for constitutional laws and regulations that are so typical of superhero exploits. In order to save democracy, these figures constantly break its rules; in fact, it is part of their superheroic quality that they do not need to obey those rules, which are, one must conclude, only meant to keep weaklings and cowards in check. The superheroes carry their own law within them. This implies that they are always guiltless and innocent, however bloody their violence may be.

Again, this mythical construct is closely related to the winner-loser dichotomy we have discussed above. The winners are above and beyond the laws and rules by which societies are ordered. It is an element of their exalted state that they take the law into their own hands. I call this the "heroic illusion": it suggests a kind of innocence that prevents any moral argument, even in the face of the most violent power plays of the "number ones" and those who try to imitate them. Again, this is by no means only an American game; it dominates the street fights of youth gangs in Central and South America and the "low intensity warfare" of warlords and mafia cartels around the globe.

The Winner-Loser Syndrome and the Religious Right: A New Syncretism

Jewett and Lawrence point out that the American version of the monomythic superhero is grounded in the Judaeo-Christian narratives of community redemption. Superheroes such as Neo in *The Matrix* are variations of the Christ figure, but with a "gospel message" markedly different from the biblical one. The point that concerns me most is that what we encounter here is an interesting — yet irritating — example of syncretism: that is, a mélange of Christian and non-Christian images and ideas. I wish to emphasize that I am not overly concerned about religious syncretism, as long as it is understood as a phenomenon that is both unavoidable and constantly in need of self-critical appraisal. Wherever the Christian faith — or any other religion, for that matter — has taken root, it has to some extent absorbed the cultural habits and religious traditions of its cultural context. But the process of syncretism becomes dangerous when its reality is being denied: in other words, when and where religious communities claim that their message is the "pure" ancestral faith, the "orthodox" representation of the foundational message, then syncretism borders on heresy.

I have observed that conservative evangelical movements, including those with a strictly apocalyptic message, are deeply influenced by these modern quasi-religious "winner" ideologies, though the movements' members insist that they are nothing but purely biblical in their orientation. As a matter of fact, it is this claim of orthodoxy that prevents them from seeing how deeply their faith has been invaded by contemporary, neoreligious winner-loser dichotomies. I suggest three areas in which this syncretistic mélange can be most easily detected.

"Get on the Winning Team with Jesus"[16]

This is the kind of slogan that is popular among evangelicals in the United States. What kind of Jesus does this preacher have in mind? The Gospels speak of a wandering rabbi who said of himself, "Foxes have holes, and birds of the air have nests, but the Son of man has nowhere to lay his head" (Matt. 8:20). This Jesus was an outsider and a friend of outsiders. His compassion led him to seek out those who lived in misery, so that he became the hope of the poor and outcast. His radical nonviolence and disarming love made him a threat to the religious leaders of his day and a potential revolutionary (even a potential terrorist!) to the Roman occupation forces. So they crucified him. To execute someone on a cross, naked and ridiculed, in the midday sun of Jerusalem — this was the cruelest way to crush a man and his ideas. This death by execution was considered to be the sign that Jesus had failed completely. Even his disciples thought so.

A few days later, the crucified one revealed himself to them as the one whose compassion had overcome even the limits of death. It was

16. "Faith Takes Center Stage at Superbowl," Associated Press, February 5, 2005. http://www.foxnews.com/story/0,2933,146507,00.html

the love that could not be crushed by the powers of death that expressed his messianic quality. So the "loser" manifested himself as the Messiah. But he made certain that being "on his team" meant walking in his steps and expecting nothing else, or better, than what had been his earthly fate. What the messianic message means is best summed up in the Sermon on the Mount (Matt. 5–7). The commitment of messianic discipleship is clearly described by the apostle Paul when he writes to the Christians in Corinth:

> To the present hour we hunger and thirst, we are ill-clad and buffeted and homeless, we labor, working with our own hands. When reviled, we bless; when persecuted, we endure; when slandered, we try to conciliate; we have become, and are now, as the refuse of the world, the offscouring of all things (1 Cor. 4:11-12).

Is this what American evangelists mean when they suggest that with Jesus we would always be on the winning team? Hardly. It is more likely that they are referring to the risen Christ, who sits "at the right hand of God, from whence he will come to judge the living and the dead," as the Apostles' Creed says. Moreover, if we recall the apocalyptic scenarios of the *Left Behind* type, Jesus has lost all his earthly characteristics. It is no longer his limitless compassion that inspires people to follow him, but the angry "super-superhero" who annihilates his adversaries in the final battles of Armageddon. Mel Gibson's film *The Passion of the Christ* (2004) presents a messiah whose superheroic endurance of unspeakable tortures on Golgotha gives him the divine "right" to become the ultimate avenger — for all those who were foolish enough not to accept his sacrificial suffering as their atonement. All the masses who have rejected him are doomed to be the losers.

One need not subscribe to the apocalyptic scenarios to confuse the seductive promises of the "winning-team" thinking with the biblical account. Ted Haggard, senior pastor of the New Life Church in Colorado Springs, Colorado, and chairman of the National Association of Evangelicals, provided a perfect example when he told a German journalist: "God helps those who help themselves. Why should we steal [money] from the rich and give [it] to the poor? Then we would have conditions like yours in Germany!"[17] I doubt that this is really the message of the Gospels, to say the least. I sympathize with the almost exasperated sigh with which Jim Wallis begins his book *God's Politics* (2005):

> Many of us feel that our faith has been stolen, and it's time to take it back. In particular, an enormous public misrepresentation of Christianity has taken place. And because of an almost uniform media misperception, many people around the world now think Christian faith stands for political commitments that are almost opposite of its true meaning. How did the faith of Jesus come to be known as pro-rich, pro-war, and only pro-American? What has happened here? And how do we get back to a historically biblical, and *genuinely* evangelical faith rescued from its contemporary distortions?[18]

What *has* happened here? I believe that one answer to Wallis's question lies in the unacknowledged syncretistic mixture of evangelical — and, more specifically, apocalyptic — fundamentalism and superhero popular culture. Although evangelists and pastors such as Ted Haggard claim that they are nothing but faithful interpreters of the Bible, they are in fact deeply influenced by the superhero fantasies surrounding them. Their Christ has nothing in common with the Christ of the Gospels; rather, he resembles the superhero who must come back to destroy those who have thrown the world into chaos. This is definitely a Christ who is pro-rich, pro-war, pro-American — in short, "good news" to the wealthy and powerful.

Today's megachurches have more in common with today's shopping malls than with the small house churches where the first Christians assembled. (It is also true, of course, that the splendid gothic cathedrals of France have nothing to do with those early house churches

---

17. Lars Jensen, "Beten bis zum Umfallen," *Süddeutsche Zeitung* 38 (Sept. 23, 2005): 34 [translated by the author].

18. Wallis, *God's Politics* (San Francisco: HarperSanFrancisco, 2005), p. 3.

either.) "One-stop worshiping" and "one-stop shopping" are products of the same consumerist mindset, and the pastors of the megachurches are self-made men in the worship-entertainment business. Is this too stark a statement? Am I simply expressing my envy as a retired minister in the Lutheran Church, a church whose numbers, like those of many other mainline churches in America, are dwindling? Am I a sore loser who cannot stand the fact that others are more successful?

I think there's more to it than that. While I am convinced that the traditional churches could learn a great deal from some of the fresh approaches elaborated in the megachurches, I am equally convinced that the "bigger is better" model does not express the core of the gospel of Jesus Christ. The self-styled pastors of the megachurches are claiming that they possess a direct entry to the mysteries of God, whereas the Orthodox churches, the Roman Catholic Church, and the churches of the Reformation hold to the conviction that the "communion of saints" requires a constant appropriation of God's word (though their methods to achieve this, of course, vary considerably). They share the view that something like a synodical, or conciliar, structure is required to sustain this self-critical discourse. They also agree, though at times with great reservation, that independent academic theological inquiry is indispensable to keep this discourse in motion. All this is based on the insight that those who claim to possess the truth are most likely to fall into the trap of triumphalist deception.

The Threat of Falling from Grace

When born-again Christians have made it to the "winning team," their ultimate concern must be to stay there. They dare never fall from grace. So they must be ready to offer — and to claim — sacrifices: they will submit all aspects of their lives and their work to the call, or the "voice," of God. Faithfulness becomes utterly important, for if they fail to do what they perceive to be God's will, they will lose the favor of the Almighty. To suffer defeat would imply to be cut from the winning team. To be a loser in the eyes of the Lord would be tantamount to final condemnation.

Such a disposition is not without risks. People in leadership positions will be tempted to interpret every difficult problem as a test of faithfulness that leaves no room for a variety of options. Therefore, the either-or dichotomy becomes the dominant mode of judging issues and persons; it creates a climate of steady insecurity that needs to be assuaged by constant control. Such persons need to demonstrate strength and determination, even in situations in which some measure of restraint would be wiser. More important, they need to stick to a decision, because to change it could provoke the spectre of being a loser, both in the eyes of the people and — far more ominously — in the eyes of God.

I admit that this perspective has helped me understand how President George W. Bush conducts his office, and the Iraq war is a telling example. Although there were many experts inside and outside the United States who advised him not to engage in such a perilous venture, he went ahead. In extensive interviews with Robert Woodward (for the latter's book *Plan of Attack*), he describes rejecting the advice of counselors such as his own father: "You know, he is the wrong father to appeal to in terms of strength. There is a higher Father that I appeal to," he said for Woodward's tape recorder.[19] It would appear from this statement that the younger Bush felt called by God to engage in this war; and thus it would have been a betrayal of a divine command if he had decided not to attack Iraq. As he prosecuted the war, he reported that he felt not the slightest hesitation: "I haven't suffered doubt . . . not at all."[20] At the same time, the president may have felt that he had to affirm himself as a strong and unwavering man: simultaneously the faithful servant and the unfailing winner. He was eager, for example, to announce triumphantly from the deck of the *Abraham Lincoln* aircraft carrier that a world historical victory had been achieved: "In the image of the falling statues [in Baghdad], we have witnessed the arrival of a new era. . . . We have seen the turning of the tide."[21] The same pattern, though at a far more trivial level, can be ob-

19. Woodward, *Plan of Attack* (New York: Simon & Schuster, 2004), p. 421.
20. Woodward, *Plan*, p. 420.
21. Woodward, *Plan*, p. 412.

served in the manner in which this president went ahead, circumventing the Senate, to appoint John Bolton to be U.S. ambassador to the United Nations. Not only did he show little respect for the grave doubts expressed in the Senate hearings; he also risked damage to his candidate's effectiveness among peers and jeopardized the standing of the United States at the United Nations. He doubtless regarded his backdoor appointment of Bolton as a victory for his higher, heroic principles.

Again, we are faced with a subtle syncretism of conservative Christianity and the winner complex of popular culture. To put it differently, the monomythical figure of the superhero shapes — and distorts, I would add — the realism of the Christian faith. The heroic illusion of the winner subverts a Christian realism that acknowledges the frailty and sinfulness even of the most ardent believer. Therefore, the apostle Paul, who had ample reason to consider himself a very successful missionary, insists on God's message: "My grace is sufficient for you, for my power is made perfect in weakness" (2 Cor. 12:9). This is the realism of grace that accepts the contradictions of human beings, while at the same time it provides them with the promise of repentance and new beginnings, with wide spaces to correct errors, work out fresh approaches, and seek sustainable ways of getting along with the other, even with enemies.

In contrast, the superhero-Christians need to be on constant alert. They cannot make peace with human frailty and vulnerability; instead, they will regard them as temptations of the evil one. They need to make sure that they are on the right side. And since they dare not acknowledge their own doubts, weaknesses, and sins, they will identify those things outside of themselves — in the other. So the world becomes full of enemies. The war against the enemies from within cannot be won; thus it needs to be fought on the external front. The result is more hostility, more suspicion, more anger, a mentality that promises "safe" conditions while it demonizes the outside world.

Headed for War

The combination of the winner-loser syndrome and the either-or scenarios of radicalized religion creates a warlike climate that is threatening to break societies apart. We see this in countries of the Middle East, where radical Muslim groups attack their more moderate compatriots. In Iraq the tensions between Sunnis and Shiites erupt in bloody attacks, to the point that the integrity of that country is in danger.

In a similar way, the tensions between right-wing Christian groups and those they regard as "liberal" or "secular" in U.S. society are increasing — and becoming increasingly bitter. The result is a culture war that threatens to divide families, neighborhoods, churches, and social organizations. "Never in my lifetime have I seen such a degree of polarization, such a heat, and so little civility and willingness to listen to other points of view. It's true from the U.S. Congress down to the small rural county in which I live," says John Graham, director of the Giraffe Project.[22] This is not good news for a nation that spends so much money on "homeland security."

At the international level, the winner-loser syndrome tends to narrow the space in which political solutions can be found. The war on terrorism and the pre-emptive, "preventive" war against Iraq have created dead-end situations. As I write this, there is little hope that Iraq will manage to preserve its territorial integrity and that the United States will be able to leave that country in an honorable manner. President Bush has repeatedly insisted that the only acceptable outcome in Iraq is "total victory," as if every aggrieved and hostile heart can somehow be converted through the application of relentless American military power.[23] The desperate determination to leave that battlefield as a winner makes more subtle political solutions impossible.

This war against terrorism has a dramatic influence on the security

22. John Graham, "America Today," remarks at a meeting of the International Council of Initiatives for Change, Vancouver, B.C., Canada (March 12, 2005, unpublished manuscript), p. 4.

23. See, for example, "Bush: U.S. Seeks Total Victory Over Terrorists," Armed Forces Information Service of the U.S. Department of Defense (online): http://www.defenselink.mil/news/Aug2005/20050822_2504.html (accessed Nov. 20, 2005).

it pretends to defend worldwide. The political climate has become one of suspicion and hostility — so much so, that official state visits or summit meetings require an amount of security measures unseen in previous times. Terrorist attacks in Madrid, London, Istanbul, and Amman have contributed to a preoccupation with security measures that reduce and imperil the civil liberties of which democratic societies are justly proud and which they seek to defend. On the other hand, the youth revolts in the towns that fringe Paris and other French cities in the fall of 2005 exemplify the deep-seated frustration of people who are the "losers" in French society. Violence appears to be the only language in which they can make themselves understood. I am sure that we will see more of this in other parts of the world.

The winner-loser dichotomy has become the rule by which the "global players" are playing their games. Again, I am not talking about the United States alone, although its superpower status makes it the dominant figure in this "team of winners." The second-tier nations of Europe and Asia belong to it as well. John Graham tells the story of himself as a young college graduate, back in the early 1960s, tramping around the world with a few dollars in his pocket. Wherever he went he was welcome. People would invite him into their homes. He had no problems finding jobs to finance his journey. He was the young American whom people around the globe liked to have around. "What has happened to us?" he says. "Forty years later, a young American college graduate will be met with suspicion and hatred wherever he goes. Back then I used to feel safe in places where a young American of today would be killed."[24]

To echo Jim Wallis's question once again, what has happened? The "American way of life" that attracted me when I was a youth has lost a good deal of its appeal. To be sure, the phenomenon of women and men trying to get to the United States in huge numbers continues to the present day, while others risk their lives to get to the wealthy nations of Europe. Compared to the misery and hopelessness of their home countries, the rich nations in North America and in Europe continue to look like "the land of the free and the home of the brave," and this

24. In a personal conversation with the author.

mythical promise is still attractive. At the same time, however, more and more people in Latin America, Africa, and Asia are finding out that this myth carries with it too much illusion for them. They are being rejected and excluded: the walls and fences that separate us, the winners, from them, the masses of the losers, are getting higher and higher. And this can only mean that the world is headed for more wars.

An Interim Conclusion

A good deal more could be said — and needs to be said — for us to understand the situation in which we find ourselves. (And by "we" I mean those who profit from the wealth and liberties both in the United States and in Europe.) What I have described, however, may suffice to illustrate the dramatic change in the perception of what "America" stands for. In the first chapter I looked at the classical messianism on which the stupendous rise of the United States is founded. In the second chapter I tried to show how massively successful the apocalyptic end-time scenarios have become. I would like to suggest that they are the *radicalization of the millennial elements* within America's messianic project. The mythical figure of the superhero and the winner-loser dichotomy that I have discussed in this third chapter can be seen as the *secularization and trivialization of the exceptionalism* that is part of the American messianic project. Furthermore, I have attempted to show that these two tendencies, radicalization and trivialization, are strengthening each other. The result is that civil religion defined by Robert Bellah has become a popular syncretistic religion that embraces politically right-wing and apocalyptic communities and elements of a broader superheroic winner-loser dualism. Common characteristics of this mind-set are a mélange of a Manichaean worldview, a zealous nationalism, and an aggressive culture war.

My impression is that we are faced with grave distortions of America's messianic tradition, which leads to this question: What is there in classic messianism that lends itself to these aberrations? And what needs to be done to reform the original messianic idea?

CHAPTER 4

"Why Do They Hate Us?"

———⟳⟲———

O n October 11, 2001, one month after the attacks on the Pentagon
and the Twin Towers in New York, President Bush said: "How
do I respond when I see that in some Islamic countries there is vitriolic
hatred for America? I'll tell you how I respond: I'm amazed, I just can't
believe it because I know how good we are."[1]

Many Americans will consider this an embarrassingly simple statement. But it may be more appropriate to regard this statement not as
an indicator of intelligence but as a confession of faith. This phrase "I
know how good we are" mirrors the untroubled belief in the inherent
goodness of America that has always been a part of its messianic mission. At the same time, the pseudo-religious character of the winner-
loser dualism comes into play as well. As many Americans conceive it,
"goodness" is made up of a variety of attributes. There is the equation
of bigness with goodness: hence a nation that has established itself as
the only superpower on earth must be good, not only in terms of economic power and scientific excellence, but also in a moral sense.[2] The

1. George W. Bush, "President Holds Prime Time News Conference, October 11,
2001" (White House release: http://www.whitehouse.gov/news/releases/2001/10/
20011011-7.html [accessed Oct. 17, 2005]).

2. See Lakoff's critical interpretation of the "strict father model," the link between

myth of the American superhero comes into it as well: the proverbial American "good guy" is inherently generous, ready to sacrifice himself to support the needy — a goodness that is without blemish or guilt. According to this conceit, the figure that came to be known as the "ugly American," a malicious meddler, in the 1950s should be, on the contrary, respected — if not admired and revered. Hence it is "amazing" that there should be so much hatred around the world, and not only in "some Islamic countries." Why is this so difficult to believe? What makes it so hard to comprehend?

I think that it important to *understand this hatred* so that we can attenuate some of its massive aggressiveness and work for a restoration of more friendly relationships. It is not sufficient to say that this hatred expresses nothing more than envy and mischief on the part of those who did not make it. It is far too simple to say that it is an anticapitalist, antidemocratic, or anti-American resentment on the part of the "losers" of this world. Yet that appears to be the only reaction that David Frum and Richard Perle — both former high-level officials in the G. W. Bush administration — can think of when they say the following about European critics:

> The United States spent hundreds of billions over half a century doing things for Europe, and, inevitably, many Europeans resent it. They resent America's ability to be generous, and they resent their need for that generosity. . . . And it's probably not coincidence that the countries in Europe where anti-Americanism runs strongest are those that have the most reason to feel grateful: France, which the United States liberated; and Germany, which the United States reconstructed and protected.[3]

This statement not only reveals an appalling ignorance of post–World War II conditions in Europe and the relationship between France and

---

goodness and success and its transferral to the political level (George Lakoff, *Don't Think of an Elephant! Know Your Values and Frame the Debate* [White River Junction,VT: Chelsea Green Publishing, 2004], pp. 6ff.).

3. David Frum and Richard Perle, *An End to Evil: How to Win the War on Terror* (New York: Random House, 2003), p. 246.

Germany, on the one hand, and the respective relationships of those two countries with the United States, on the other; it also illustrates how deeply the two authors are victims of their own belief in America's superheroic goodness. They exhibit a kind of national narcissism when they go on to proclaim: "Now that the United States has become the greatest of all great powers in world history, its triumph has shown that freedom is irresistible."[4] The resulting reasoning would go that, since what the United States has done and will do is inherently righteous, the others must be wrong. And more than just wrong: they must be morally despicable. The reluctance of some Europeans to follow American military initiatives allows Frum and Perle to see a kind of moral kinship between Europeans and the terrorists: "The jealousy and resentment that animate the terrorists also affect many of our former cold war allies," as they coyly put it.[5] This is messianic superheroic "innocence" — accompanied by a bipolar moral map — carried to its arrogant and simplistic extreme.

However, the matter is far too important to be left at this shallow ideological level. Our attempt to understand the widespread hatred of the United States around the world must be more substantial. If one looks at the arguments being offered to explain this hatred and resentment, one comes across three terms: genocide, slavery, and imperialism. Any thoughtful citizen of the United States will immediately know what they refer to. *Genocide* refers to the near-extinction of the indigenous nations of the American continent, a crime of staggering proportions, but one that is far distant in time for most of us today and still beyond our comprehension. But if one takes the trouble to listen to those Native Americans who have survived — as I have done on many occasions — one encounters an abysmally deep sadness, a haunting woundedness that seems to have taken the soul out of them. For the remnants of these great nations it is an unending, unforgettably real story.

Slavery, of course, refers to the centuries-old history of subjugation of African women and men in the Americas, North and South. Al-

4. Frum and Perle, *An End to Evil,* p. 275.
5. Frum and Perle, *An End to Evil,* p. 236.

though slavery was officially abolished a century and a half ago, it lingers on. Hurricane Katrina exposed the economic and social conditions of many African-Americans, but it is not the social misery that first comes to mind. Behind that misery I sense a spiritual terror, a kind of lostness that makes many African-Americans hopeless. Their steady experience of stigmatization, repeated through many generations, has given many of them — especially the men — the feeling of being America's "born losers," an incapacitating self-image that creates apathy and a gnawing sense of futility. The upward mobility that has been typical of most ethnic groups that have immigrated to the United States seems, in large measure, to bypass many in African-American communities.

Third, *imperialism* is a term that people in Central and South America, in the Philippines and elsewhere in Asia, and not least in the Middle East, use to describe what the United States signifies for them. It begins with the "doctrine" of "America for the Americans," which was set forth by the fifth president of the United States in his Monroe Doctrine. There is no need to recount the details of the United States' early conquests in its own hemisphere and other parts of the world. But at the end of the Mexican War (1846-1848), Mexico was forced to cede all territories north of the Rio Grande (what is today the states of Texas, California, Nevada, New Mexico, Utah, as well as parts of Arizona and Colorado). The war for the Southwest territories was followed by the intermittent interventions and de facto occupations by the U.S. Marines of Nicaragua and Panama. As a result of the Spanish-American War (1898-1901), the United States took control of and occupied Puerto Rico, Guam, and the Philippine Islands (its annexation of this last country lasted until 1946 and included the brutal suppression of twentieth-century Filipino uprisings aimed at national autonomy). All over Latin America, U.S. governments have supported dictatorial régimes and helped to overthrow democratically elected governments (e.g., the government of Zelayo in Nicaragua in 1909, of Arbenz in Guatemala in 1954, and of Allende in Chile in 1973). Guantánamo Bay on the island of Cuba has been the site of a U.S. base since 1903.

If one adds to this history the overthrow of the Mossadekh government of Iran in 1954 and the ensuing support for Shah Reza Pahlevi's dictatorial rule; and the U.S. support for Iraq's Saddam Hussein in his war against Iran (before he fell from favor with the U.S.) — it is not difficult to imagine how Middle Easterners might see the two wars against Iraq, led by Presidents Bush Sr. and Bush Jr., as the latest examples of an imperialist tradition. I do not say that one has to see it in this way. My point is simply that, for the victims, the expanding geographical scope of U.S. invasions, even when American leaders label them as "liberations" in "the march of freedom," can be regarded as one grand strategy for expansive control of the entire world.

It is easy, of course, for historians to show how the terms "genocide," "slavery," and "imperialism" hardly suffice to satisfactorily describe the complexities of the American conquest, first of the North American continent and then beyond. One needs to remember that these conquests are tied together with companion conquests in which the European powers competed for the control of the world in the nineteenth and early twentieth centuries. Furthermore, it is easy — and necessary — to highlight the impressive debate and dissent within the United States that have accompanied these political and military developments. The wealthy steel magnate Andrew Carnegie, for example, was so distressed by the U.S. suppression of freedom in the Philippines that he offered President McKinley twenty million dollars (the treaty price with Spain) so that the country could be returned to control of its own independence movement. However, "objective" scientific and historical reasoning is of little avail when it comes to understanding the feelings of the victims and the lasting impact of their traumatization. Carnegie's generous offer failed, and what is thus at stake is not who was "right" or "wrong" or what the balancing complexities were or are in such situations, but the actual experiences and the manner in which people *remember* them. It is little consolation to the hundreds of thousands of Filipinos who died resisting American control that there were politically ineffective sympathizers within the U.S. that supported their autonomy.[6]

6. The course of the Philippine Insurrection and the role of anti-imperialists in opposing it is told in many sources, including Walter LaFeber, *The American Age: U.S. Foreign Policy at Home and Abroad, 1750 to Present* (New York: W. W. Norton, 1989).

Selective Remembering:
The Hermeneutics of Humiliation and Denial

It is often said that the winners not only make history, they also decide what is to be remembered and what is to be forgotten. But memories cannot be ordered around like that. They have subtle ways of staying alive, and if they are not handled with care, they can have a haunting impact on the present. To begin with, all acts of gross injustice, such as crimes, massacres, or wars, establish a *dual history of remembering*. For the perpetrators it is, simply put, a history of guilt and shame; for those on the victim side, it is a history of humiliation and hurt. I believe that it is easier to live with memories of guilt than with memories of humiliation. While the former is an abuse of power that does not diminish the potential to act, the latter is an experience of suffering that borders on an impairment of the self.

These dual histories form a chain that locks both sides to the past and to each other, mostly in unconscious — and thus mutually irritating — ways.

My impression is that the "vitriolic hatred" that President Bush spoke of in his October 2001 speech is an expression, and an unfortunate result, of this "chain of memories." The president decided that the only way to destroy this "chain" was to go to war "to eradicate terrorism at its root."[7] But what he achieved was to forge that chain of hatred to be longer than it was before, and its links to be heavier. Can this chain be unlocked? I am convinced that it can be — but certainly not by retaliation, for that is nothing but a reactive repetition of the evil it pretends to overcome. Retaliation only prolongs the bondage to a hostile polarity, while reconciliation, though much despised and ridiculed by the world's "tough guys," is a creative way to liberate both parties from the lasting impact of past injustices. It is possible for human beings to heal their enervating memories. Long-time enemies can become good neighbors and trusted friends. But this is a process that requires a kind of strength and

---

7. "National Strategy for Combating Terrorism" (White House Press release, Feb. 2003: http://www.whitehouse.gov/news/releases/2003/02/counter_terrorism/introduction.pdf [accessed Sept. 28, 2005]).

courage that most of the "winners" do not possess.[8] I will say more about this "art of remembering" in the chapters that follow.

The Hermeneutics of Humiliation

I am still concerned with understanding the poisonous hatred against the United States that can be found not only in so many places around the globe but also within the United States itself. We will have to look at both sides of the "chain." Looking first at the victim side, it is obvious that hatred, resentment, and suspicion are products of various ways in which experiences of traumatization and humiliation are being kept alive or, rather, are keeping themselves alive. Therefore, it will not suffice to simply say that remembering is a construction of past events as if it were a matter of conscious decision alone. The intriguing and disturbing thing is that subconscious motives play their vexing role in the formation of a narrative that keeps the hurtful experiences alive. We are faced with a phenomenon that could be called "hermeneutics of humiliation." I will mention here just three aspects: (1) A great deal of the hatred against America that one encounters around the world has to do with the *feeling*[9] of many people that their *suffering has not been duly acknowledged.* They are under the infuriating impression that their dignity has been crushed and their sovereignty as human beings and as nations has been trampled on. They resent the arrogance of power, the crushing superiority that reduces them to what seems a subhuman level of impotence. It is, so to speak, an emasculating experience that undercuts the sense of self. One staining legacy of America is its long history of domestic terrorism against blacks. It was a series of terrifying murders that left some 3,500 dead in ritual executions.[10] As Joseph S. Tuman described

8. I have described these processes of reconciliation in greater detail in Müller-Fahrenholz, *The Art of Forgiveness: Theological Reflections on Healing and Reconciliation* (Geneva: WCC Publications, 1997).

9. I use the term "feeling" because it points to the visceral "gut level" at which strong impulses such as hatred are located and nourished. Remembering is more a matter of feeling than of reflection, of amorphous instinct rather than critical insight.

10. Robert L. Zangrando, "Lynching," in *The Reader's Companion to American History,* Eric Foner and John A. Garraty, eds. (New York: Houghton Mifflin, 1991).

"the message" in his *Communicating Terror,* the white sheets and burning crosses of the Ku Klux Klan "were symbols of death, injury, serious destruction. Seeing them in the context of lynching, flogging, castration, shooting, stabbing, beating, and burning only reinforced this symbolism."[11] The Klan is now rather quiet, but how could such experiences be forgotten by those linked to the victims?

This feeling of a burning wrong cries out for justice, but there is no justice big enough to redeem a broken self. It cries out for revenge, but senses in advance the futility of it. All this arouses feelings of profound rage, for which there is no outlet because the enemy is far too big to be seriously hurt. So frustration and fury become intertwined. Life appears to have no meaning because failure is always on the personal horizon; hence a life can just as well be sacrificed in a suicide attack or wasted in self-destructive indolence.

(2) A way out of this inner turmoil is to blame everything on the powerful "gringo." He becomes responsible for all things, even for those things the "victim" could easily take care of himself. The gringo is seen to be behind everything — manipulating, maneuvering, and dominating the victimized at will. Scapegoating and witch-hunting can thus become part of the game to regain some sense of standing. For if one cannot confront the enemy himself, one can vent one's anger at some of his "collaborators" (at this writing, suicide attacks in Iraq are often aimed at Iraqi policemen in the belief that they are "collaborating" with the enemy).

(3) It is part of the hermeneutics of humiliation to construct a distorted image of the "enemy." The Lebanese writer Amin Maalouf quotes from a letter by Mehmet Ali Agca, the Turk who attempted to assassinate Pope John Paul II in May 1981: "I have decided to kill John Paul II, the Highest Commander of the Crusaders."[12] The late Edward Said makes a similar observation in the essay I have quoted above. He notes that, in most Arab countries, there exists a highly fictitious and fantastic image of the United States, almost a caricature of what it re-

11. Joseph S. Tuman, *Communicating Terror* (Thousand Oaks, CA: Sage Publications, 1998), p. 58.

12. Amin Maalouf, *The Crusades Through Arab Eyes* (New York: Schocken, 1984), p. xx.

ally is. Of course, there is a certain logic to it, because the reduction of one's own self-image is accompanied by a distorted image of the perceived all-powerful one that leaves little room for distinctions or nuance. It is as though one lived in a frozen history. The weaker culture uses age-old paradigms and images again and again to "understand" new developments. I have seen this in Latin America as well. One can find a kind of demonization that prevents people from acknowledging the differences within the United States and renders them unable to appreciate self-critical views that many Americans hold regarding the government's policies. Allowing space for varied approaches would upset the "image of the enemy."

It is only one further step to give this demonization a religous form by turning it into satanization. Those who call the United States the "(great) Satan" create a metaphysical gap between themselves and the enemy that can never be overcome. In fact, no pious victim should even *wish* to overcome it. Denouncing the United States as the incorporation of all evil exempts those who believe it from the responsibility to seek ways of solving the problem. Once a conflict has been carried to such a metahistorical extreme, there can be no prospect of ever solving it by earthly means. Enmity becomes total — a "law" of history.

The Hermeneutics of Denial

What about the remembering on the side of the victors? My impression is that the official narrative of the United States is dominated by a sense of success and even triumph. A broad and sweeping look at the history of the United States, from its tiny beginnings to its status as the world's only superpower, suggests nothing but unstoppable progress and — in religious terms — proof of divine blessing and providential exceptionality. What does this metanarrative do to its cruel underside, to the legacies of genocide, slavery, and imperialist conquest? The predominant reaction can be seen as one of denial.[13] How does it work?

13. How difficult it is to arrive at an honest evaluation of the evils hidden in the past of the United States is illustrated in the work of Donald W. Shriver, Jr. See his *Honest Patriots: Loving a Country Enough to Remember Its Misdeeds* (New York and Oxford: Oxford University Press, 2005).

The "hermeneutics of denial" has many faces, of which the following appear to me to be most important.

The first mode of denial is to declare history insignificant. This may be an instinctive reaction of people who do not wish to be reminded of age-old feelings of uprootedness. As I have suggested in the introduction to this book, the hidden pains of a disrupted life may have been turned into a general unwillingness to look at the past. If one makes history insignificant, then the study of it becomes irrelevant as well. But ignoring history is a way of avoiding the messages that may disturb our illegitimate comfort. Again, many citizens of the United States may have little inclination to take a closer look at the history of their country (even if their schooling gives them the opportunity for it), because their own story within this larger history is so short. Large immigrant groups from Asia or Latin America may see little reason to identify fully with the "genocide," "slavery," and "imperialism" part of U.S. history. Not only does it appear to be in the distant past; more significantly, they have their own experiences of discrimination to fend off. Furthermore, it's likely that they see themselves as coming to America for an opportunity, not to participate in a sense of responsibility for the legacies of a long past.

It can hardly be denied that most Americans will have neither time nor the inclination to study what the imperial conquests of the United States did to peoples on the North American continent or in distant continents. As would be true in other nations, the general public depends on the trustworthiness of its political leaders and the reliability of the educational sector and the news media in order to get clues about what their country has done, and is doing, around the globe. But one thing I do find difficult to understand is that members of the U.S. Congress have actually boasted that they do not have a passport. This must mean that they never travel abroad. And that implies that they never even care to take a personal look at those parts of the world that are profoundly affected by their decisions. This kind of willful ignorance is part of the failure to take personal responsibility for the far-reaching implications of their policies. Not caring to know is an emphatic expression of denial.

A very strong motive for denying the sinister aspects of U.S. history is the messianism inherent in the "American experiment." As we have discussed in the first chapter, this divine mission renders its messengers inherently "good" (see President Bush's statement quoted at the beginning of this chapter); this goodness implies innocence. Acts committed in the pursuit of this divine task may be "messy," but they cannot be morally wrong. To be sure, mistakes are unavoidable. The real matter is that there cannot be such a thing as corporate and national guilt. As we have discussed in the previous chapter, the myth of the American superhero implies a position beyond and above the laws by which ordinary communities are ruled. The superhero acts on behalf of his inner superior "right" and thus cannot be stopped by the legal qualms of the "losers," or indeed the qualms of those insisting on legal distinctions and procedures. This mythological construct places the hero outside the all-too-human dilemma of right and wrong. He remains innocent, however violent his acts may "need" to be. This construct is also a form of denial. It expresses the illusionary belief that "superheroic" behavior can forever remain pure and undefiled by earthly messiness. The White House legal staff, in seeking ways to evade any presidential criminal liability for approving acts of torture that violated U.S. statutes, put it this way: "In light of the President's complete authority over the conduct of war, without a clear statement otherwise, we will not read a criminal statute as infringing on the President's ultimate authority in these areas."[14] In this construction, the hero is truly above any law — whether human or divine.

The flip side of such messianic innocence is that the enemies, the victims, must be blamed for the blood that is spilled. Those who put themselves in the way of the divinely ordained "crusade" of liberty and progress represent the "powers of darkness," even if they do not belong to an "axis of evil." The mythological construct that confers the superhero's status as innocent lays the responsibility for the sacrifices at the feet of the adversary.

This mythological framework of denial finds its metaphysical jus-

14. "Memo for Alberto O. Gonzales, Counsel to the President, Aug. 1, 2002." Posted by PBS/Frontline: http://news.findlaw.com/hdocs/docs/doj/bybee80102mem.pdf (the statute in question is 18 U.S.C., 18 §§ 2340-2340A).

tification in the end-time scenarios sketched out in chapter 2. Once the earthly affairs are placed within the final war between Christ and the Antichrist, the historical actors are no longer accountable for their deeds. The final accountability is with the metahistorical powers. The "hermeneutics of denial" takes its urgency from the tension between the promise of innocence and the reality of failure. In fact, the greater the claim to goodness, the more urgent the need to "undo" the memories of wrong. How this "need" works has been described by Greg Mitchell and Robert J. Lifton in their book *Hiroshima in America*.[15] Their study was inspired by the way an exhibit planned in 1995 by the Smithsonian Institute on the occasion of the fiftieth anniversary of the atomic bombing of Hiroshima had been suppressed and officially censored. The Smithsonian's original plan included not only the display of the *Enola Gay,* the plane that carried the atomic bomb to the Japanese cities, and the documentation of the decisions connected to this ominous flight. Curators also wanted to illustrate the effects of the bomb at "ground zero"; in other words, they wanted to present the horrifying pictures of devastation and human suffering on the part of the Japanese.

The war veterans' asssociations and influential segments of the Clinton administration[16] intervened to make sure that this exhibit would not be mounted as planned. Lifton and Mitchell say:

> From the start [of the atomic age], Americans were not shown the human effects of the bomb. This reinforced the psychological resistance to taking in the horror of Hiroshima. Nearly fifty years later, the same impulses were at play in the Smithsonian dispute. Curators, under pressure, removed from the exhibit nearly every photograph of dead or badly injured Japanese civilians. There remains today a reluctance to face squarely what America did, or excuse it, perhaps even to wish it away.[17]

15. Robert Jay Lifton and Greg Mitchell, *Hiroshima in America: Fifty Years of Denial* (New York: G. P. Putnam, 1995).

16. Lifton and Mitchell, *Hiroshima,* pp. 288, 295.

17. Lifton and Mitchell, *Hiroshima,* p. xv.

It is this mixture of reluctance, self-pardon, and wishful thinking that characterizes denial. Mitchell and Lifton argue that Hiroshima maintains a haunting presence because it reminds Americans of their profound dilemma: that a nation proud of its goodness and decency should have committed an unprecedented crime, a crime that used weapons of "mass destruction" against hundreds of thousands of *unarmed* Japanese citizens. Lifton and Mitchell continue:

> We had done something that seemed to endanger the whole world. Such feelings of self-accusation were rendered equally painful by our sense of ourselves as a people of special goodness, indeed as a people living always in God's grace. However illusory, this national self-image automatically raised questions of good and evil: "If we have struggled to bring about a Kingdom of Heaven on earth, we have been willing to borrow our tools from the Kingdom of Hell," as one observer put it. Our very claim to virtue can thus contribute to a sense of spiritual fall, all the more so in perceiving the inability of our religious and political leaders to help us look at the dark moral questions.[18]

For the psychologist Lifton, one of the most alarming expressions of denial is that the deadly power of the nuclear bomb can be — and has been — transformed into an object of desire and idolized as an instrument of redemption.

In the hermeneutics of denial, destruction becomes the ultimate "solution": it means embracing the bomb because of its utter deadliness, revering it for its power to annihilate all things — a power hitherto reserved to God alone. This is a point where apocalyptic end-time scenarios can be fused with images of nuclear destruction; the thing to be most feared becomes the thing to be most desired.[19]

18. Lifton and Mitchell, *Hiroshima*, p. 309.

19. Lifton has called this faith "nuclearism"; see Robert J. Lifton and Richard Falk, *Indefensible Weapons: The Political and Psychological Case Against Nuclearism* (New York: Basic Books, 1982). See also Robert Jay Lifton, *The Broken Connection: On Death and the Continuity of Life* (New York: Basic Books, 1983), pp. 369-87; and Lifton,

For the Grace of God: Deep Remembering

"Why do they hate us?" This is the question to which I've been trying to respond. The first observation was that every great crime produces a dual history, a history of repressed guilt/shame/remorse, and a history of unredeemed humiliation and hurt. This has led to the notion that these "histories" produce their own "hermeneutics," that is, a process of interpretation that produces what is also called its specific "narrative." This is the way families construct specific stories of the hurts they have had to suffer. Nations establish complex legends and myths around events that have occurred centuries ago. For instance, in a long process of historical interpretation, as I have mentioned, Serbians have created a myth of national victimhood for themselves based on an event that occurred over six centuries ago: the Battle of the Kosovo (1389), in which a Serbian army was defeated by the advancing Ottoman Empire. They saw themselves defending a Christian Europe, which never reciprocated with adequate gratitude. I have met people in Ireland who have spoken to me about what Oliver Cromwell did "to us" — as if this happened yesterday (Cromwell invaded Ireland in 1649)! This is a hermeneutics of humiliation, and a comparable form of it can be found in Arab countries, where the aggrieved interpret the steady decline of the once-great Muslim Empire as something that came about only because of external "crusading" forces.

On the other hand, I think that the myth-makers in America have developed a hermeneutics of denial, which focuses on America's unstoppable rise as the world's superpower, while it tries to ignore the violence that has assisted it in attaining that status. Both kinds of hermeneutics exemplify selective remembering. Although this may sound academic, it is of utmost relevance to the ways people and nations think about and relate to each other. For even while we can distinguish between a hermeneutics of humiliation and a hermeneutics of denial, we need to be aware that both of them remain part of the chain that binds some nations together in antagonism. As a matter of fact, they

---

Superpower Syndrome: America's Apocalyptic Confrontation with the World (New York: Thunder's Mouth Press/Nation Books, 2003).

constantly reconstruct and strengthen its links. As much as the perpe-trators and the victims would like to be independent of each other, this "chain" keeps them locked in a frightening — and often deadly — embrace.

Selective remembering, then, sustains and empowers an *ongoing process of "dis-memberment."* Suspicion and distrust, animosity and hatred form the primordial soup that constantly poisons the encoun-ters between countries that are tied to their distinctive interpretations of history. For instance, relationships between Ireland and Great Brit-ain have remained strained for decades: though both are members of the European Community, their age-old animosities and prejudices have not been laid to rest. Another example is the situation in the for-mer Yugoslavia. While that combined country lasted, from 1946 to 1991, the forceful histories of hatred could be kept at bay; but it ex-ploded as soon as Yugoslavia broke apart into secessionist republics in 1991-92. Now it takes massive outside pressure to create some kind of precarious space in which the Serbs, the Croats, the Bosnians, and the Albanians can live side by side. Their history of dis-memberment pre-vents them from really living together.

I refer to these European examples in order to show that the ha-tred and resentment that so many people around the world have to-ward the United States today is not a singular phenomenon in any way. But it is singularly dangerous, just because the confrontational power residing in such dis-memberment processes is so great.

Why, then, is there so much hatred? My point is that, by looking at the hermeneutical components of humiliation and denial, we begin to get a feeling for the "logic of misunderstanding" that keeps the dis-memberment and its centripetal forces alive. This logic colors every-thing that some people of the Middle East hear concerning their status as a people. Thus, when these people hear President George W. Bush speak about "democracy," they hear him talking about their own op-pression. When he talks about "liberty," they hear him talking about Abu Ghraib. In the logic of misunderstanding, words and concepts ac-quire different — if not opposite — meanings that express the stakes and the history of hopes or grievances associated with the relationship.

The same is true on the side of the United States: the hermeneutics of denial prevents it from really seeing the impact of its power on pow-erless peoples or nations, and prevents it from getting a feeling for their specific needs and goals. It aggravates the discrepancies and distortions in the political agenda. Therefore, it makes sense to assume that Amer-ica felt "dis-membered" by the assault of 9/11: this feeling was based on the comfortable illusion of living in an invulnerable space outside and above the rest of humanity. Obviously, we are not simply talking about words or concepts. The "logic of misunderstanding" leads to misinfor-mation and misdeeds. Former President Jimmy Carter's article in the *Los Angeles Times*, "This Isn't the Real America," is eloquent proof of the growing discrepancy between the classic self-image of the United States "as the unswerving champion of peace, freedom and human rights" and the Bush administration's disregard of the Geneva Conven-tion of 1949 regarding prisoners of war, not to mention its open support for torture in Iraq, Afghanistan, Guantánamo, and elsewhere.[20] Former President Carter gives many more examples that need not be repeated here. His anguished statement is mirrored by an observation from the well-known German social philosopher Jürgen Habermas: "The nor-mative authority of America lies in shambles."[21]

The point I want to make is that the age-old processes of dis-memberment should not be underestimated. Their destructive might propels the downward spiral of violence that keeps perpetrators and victims, "winners" and "losers," tied together. Its latest manifestation is the global war on terrorism: more and more people realize that this is a "war" that cannot be won; it is a dead end in the truest sense of the word.

What can be done to overcome the self-destructive processes of "dis-membering"? I believe that the answer is deep remembering.[22] I

---

20. Jimmy Carter, "This Isn't the Real America," *Los Angeles Times* (Nov. 14, 2005). See Carter's recent book, *Our Endangered Values: America's Moral Crisis* (New York: Simon & Schuster, 2005).

21. Jürgen Habermas, in the *Frankfurter Allgemeine Zeitung*, Apr. 17, 2003 (quoted by Hans-Eckehard Bahr, *Erbarmen mit Amerika: Deutsche Alternativen* [Berlin: Aufbau-Verlag, 2003], p. 50).

22. Müller-Fahrenholz, *The Art of Forgiveness*, Part Two: "Deep Remembering in Politics and Public Life," pp. 42-101.

should clarify this by saying that here I am taking the verb "to remember" in its original meaning — literally "re-member" — to express the act of putting back together members that have been severed. Re-membering is much more than the studying of past events; it is about connecting ourselves to the events and processes that have made up the conditions in which we exist. Deep remembering, of course, implies that we must include the dark aspects of our history. We need to look squarely at those things we would wish to forget, because those are precisely the aspects that do not fit nicely into the image we would love to have of ourselves. Crimes, massacres, systems of oppression, and contempt — we need to re-member these sinister aspects of our past along with the constructive and fruitful aspects of our national life and history.

I am not interested in self-flagellation; rather, I am searching for memory strategies that may constructively connect us to both our good and dark legacies. Taking deep remembering seriously will enable us to include the others, the strangers, even our enemies, and to become mindful of their strengths and failures. Re-membering and re-connecting are related: the past becomes an integral part of our present condition. This is a process that allows us to overcome the disruptive processes of dis-membering. While denial chains people to the past, deep remembering is a way — though a painful one — for them to liberate themselves from this captivity and to arrive at a more honest awareness of the others and of themselves.

I think it is fair to say that my country has become engaged in this work of deep remembering. Germany has tried hard to face up to the crimes of Hitler and the Wehrmacht, to the horrors of the Holocaust.[23] I am not saying that Germans engaged in this process unanimously, or that it is complete. In fact, there can be no end to re-membering; it is an ongoing task. This is the context from which I suggest that such an understanding of deep remembering might be applied to the United States. My suggestion echoes the question of Donald W. Shriver, Jr.:

23. For years an extensive exhibit that was entitled "Crimes of the Wehrmacht" toured German cities and was also shown in other countries. A broader picture is presented by Donald W. Shriver, Jr., in *Honest Patriots:* its first part (pp. 15-61) is entitled "Germany Remembers."

"Is there a formula for combining civic shame with civic pride to yield an honest patriotism?"[24]

My observations in the first three chapters regarding American messianism, its apocalyptic distortions, and its superheroic trivializations lead me to the conclusion that there needs to be a way of connecting greatness and guilt, progress and failure. It is possible to live in God's grace and at the same time to honestly confront the evil that has been done. The messianic claims to goodness must be reconciled with the atrocities committed. This may appear to be impossible. But my response as a Christian is that it is not only possible, but is in fact inevitable, that we live in the grace of God and still fall from grace. This is the real power of the Christian faith: that the grace of God is great enough to accept the sinfulness of human beings and to offer them the chance to change their ways. This is what repentance and conversion are about. There is an old rabbinic saying that expresses this: "Before God made creation he created the *teshuba*" (the Hebrew word for "change" and "conversion"). In other words, the possibility of changing perceptions and patterns of behavior, of repenting for evil acts, and of seeking ways to alleviate their disastrous impact — all of this is built into God's creation. Determinism and fatalism are incompatible with the grace of God; new beginnings are possible. No dead end is too narrow to prevent us from turning around.

To those who find this excessively pious, let me quote from the secular psychologist Robert Jay Lifton:

> The healthier alternative is an acceptance of some measure of ambiguity, of inevitable elements of confusion and contradiction, whether in relation to large historical events or in matters of personal experience. . . . It is often claimed that no such acceptance of ambiguity is possible because superpowers, like nations, like people, are uncomfortable with it. . . . Ambiguity, in fact, is central to human function, recognized and provided for by cultural institutions and practices everywhere.[25]

24. Shriver, *Honest Patriots*, p. 61.
25. Lifton, *Superpower Syndrome*, pp. 196f.

The secular language of the psychologist, however, does not suffice. "Ambiguity" is not clear enough to express the profound moral dilemma in which human beings, nations, and superpowers find themselves when they are confronted with the fact that *deliberate evil* has been done. This is a reality that is often confused with "errors" or "mistakes." But, while the latter are committed involuntarily, the former is a product of conscious intent and deliberate planning. To be sure, mistakes can have disastrous effects, yet their moral impact differs from that of evil acts. For this deliberate and intentional evil I have used the term "guilt" on various occasions. But it is not difficult to hear citizens of the United States asking these indignant questions: "How can I be guilty of genocidally motivated crimes against the Native American peoples? Or of slavery? All this happened decades or centuries before I was born! How can I be held responsible for the imperialist conquests of the United States in foreign lands? If there were atrocities, how was I to know — or to blame?" So an explanatory comment may be appropriate here.

In 1946, one year after the end of World War II, when the heinous deeds of the Nazi era began to be widely known, the German philosopher Karl Jaspers started his teaching work at the University of Heidelberg with a lecture on *die Schuldfrage,* which grew into his book *The Question of German Guilt.*[26] In this widely read work, Jaspers suggested that we distinguish between four different modes of guilt.

The first one is the guilt resulting from committing criminal offenses: we could call it *criminal* guilt. It is commonly accepted that the place to deal with this kind of guilt is in the courts. There continue to be difficulties with the notion of "criminal guilt" as applied to political acts, such as wars or massacres, or clandestine activity, such as torture. Therefore, prominent Nazi leaders were brought to the Nuremberg Trials, where they were accused and convicted of crimes against humanity and related charges. The results of those proceedings have

26. Karl Jaspers, *The Question of German Guilt* (New York: Fordham University Press, 1947), published as *Die Schuldfrage* in Germany in 1946. It may be worth adding that Jaspers himself had been under severe pressure from the Nazis. After 1937 he was not permitted to lecture or to publish. A threatened deportation to a concentration camp was forestalled when the U.S. Army liberated and occupied Heidelberg.

seemed, for many decades now, to be a satisfactory way of calling human agents to accountability for their actions. Accordingly, after a difficult preparatory process, the International Criminal Court in The Hague was finally set up (in March 2003) as an international forum before which similar crimes can be brought. But until now, the United States has refused to become a member of this court, even though American judges were prominent in the Nuremberg Trials and American legal experts have played leading roles in the development of international law. This refusal to cooperate is seen by many in the international community as an indication that the United States takes the "right" to exempt itself from the normative framework of international law.

Jaspers's second notion of guilt is *political*. It refers to acts of politicians for which the citizens are held accountable. In this category, one could place sanctions against a people as a way to punish the crimes of their leaders. The international sanctions against South Africa's apartheid régime or against the dictatorships of Saddam Hussein and Fidel Castro are ways to have the people suffer for the crimes of their leaders.

The third category for Jaspers is *moral* guilt. The "court" that speaks to this category is the conscience of each individual.

Finally, Jaspers speaks of *metaphysical* guilt. This is a concept that describes the co-responsibility of each human being for the evil that is being done. The only "court" before which we can address this guilt is God.

Can Jaspers's argument be applied to the United States? The title of the English translation of his book seems to suggest that Jaspers was exclusively referring to "German guilt." In fact, Jaspers spoke about "the question of guilt." And though the immediate context of his reflections was the Nazi era (1933-1945), it is clear to me that he was dealing with guilt as a general human condition. If not, one would have to conclude that guilt is something that can only be applied to the "losers" and not to the "winners." I believe that Jaspers's notion of guilt must be applied to all human evil, regardless of the contexts and pretexts that are used to frame it.

I am not suggesting a similarity between the United States and

Nazi Germany. Germany's guilt remains what it is — a crime of massive singularity. At the same time, the guilt of the United States remains what it is: it is written into U.S. history as the shadow side of its ascent to supremacy among the great military powers. We Germans need to confront our historical guilt in each of the four categories suggested by Jaspers. We have, in fact, done that to varying degrees — compelled, of course, by the fact that Germany was the great loser in World War II. This burden of defeat has forced us to engage in this work more deeply than other nations have had to. I should like to insist, however, that facing guilt must remain independent of victory or defeat. It is a matter pertaining to the moral sovereignty that is the core of our humanity. Thus, every citizen of the United States, just like any other citizen of any other country, needs to face his or her guilt with regard to the misdeeds committed.

According to Jaspers's categories, it would be obvious that no citizen of the United States of today is *criminally* guilty of atrocities committed by his or her ancestors. But all citizens of the United States are *politically* and *morally* responsible for the long-term effects of past evil that they allow to persist. The question of *metaphysical* guilt is of a different order, and people will respond to it according to their religious orientations. But I would want to add that the postures of the end-time apocalypticists express denial. The end-time faithful place the final responsibility for the world's evil at the feet of the Antichrist and thereby exempt some few redeemed (or "chosen") people from their earthly accountability.

At its trancendent level, the notion of guilt addresses all human beings at the core level of our commonality: it reminds all of us of our common and fundamental frailty. This reflection is by no means a pessimistic indulgence in human brokenness, with its seductive invitation to inertia. On the contrary, it embodies a connectedness that is based on honesty and truthfulness, thus opening paths for more reliable relationships.

Can the devastating processes of dis-memberment be halted? Or, to put it positively, can we move away from our confrontational hermeneutics of denial and humiliation toward a process of deep remembering that will enable us to recognize the truth about ourselves (and the enemies within ourselves) as well as about the enemies (and ourselves within the enemies)? I am convinced that we can. This conviction is based on the assumption that everything we do as individuals or as nations must begin with the acknowledgment that, as members of the human family, we are fundamentally one. This will and must be the restraining factor for the "missions" and "fortunes" that peoples and nations are forever tempted to pursue.

CHAPTER 5

9/11 — A Missed Opportunity

———◦◦◦———

After the September 11, 2001, terrorist attacks on the Pentagon and the Twin Towers, it took President Bush only six days to authorize the U.S. Army Command to prepare for war against the Al Qaeda network and the Taliban régime in Afghanistan. Equally revealing is the fact that the president, influenced by Vice President Cheney and Secretary of Defense Rumsfeld, issued the order to work out scenarios for a war against Iraq.[1] Many have said that 9/11 was a turning point in U.S. history, and it could have been. But the administration's style of reaction perpetuated an all-too-familiar pattern. Although the "war against terrorism" has some sad new components — the "right" to launch pre-emptive strikes, for instance — it is not new. It is exactly what the terrorists expected. Moreover, it mirrors, on a grossly enlarged scale, the messianic assumptions of the "redeemer nation." "To rid the world of evil" is a program that carries American messianism to new illusionary extremes.

1. Hans von Sponeck and Andreas Zumach, *Irak — Chronik eines gewollten Krieges* (Köln: Kiepenhauer und Witsch, 2003), pp. 18, 27.

94

A New Starting Point: Vulnerability

Was there an alternative? Probably not. And yet there might have been an entirely different approach: 9/11 could have been a moment of promise, what Christians sometimes refer to as *kairos,* a challenging time of turning when those who accept a faith are called on to live it in a creative way. President Bush, unashamedly Christian in his public confessions, might have led his nation in a way that reflected the gospel's potential for reconciliation and a reconstruction of world politics.

Under the immediate impact of 9/11, a different presidential ghostwriter might have had the president addressing the nation in the following way:

My Fellow Americans:

We have been hit. The attacks on the Twin Towers and the Pentagon have damaged every one of us. We are filled with anger and rage; for in two hundred years our country has never experienced such an attack from the outside.

So everything in us cries out for revenge. But should we give in to this cry? It would be the easier way. And I am sure you would support me if I mobilized our troops to hunt down the terrorists and those who helped them wherever they are hiding.

But I propose to take another route. It may baffle you — even infuriate you — at first hearing. But I ask that you consider it with care.

The assaults have shown us something we needed to know: we are vulnerable. Yes, we are an open country. We are a nation linked to other nations around the globe. Therefore, strangers can come into our country. They can hijack airplanes and steer them into high-rise buildings. Of course, we can improve our security measures. But the fact of our grave vulnerability remains.

The experience of this immense cruelty is, at the moment of such great suffering, also our moment of truth about the vulnerability that we share with others. For now we can empathize with other people who live through civil wars for years and even decades. We can now grasp how people feel when their cities

have been bombed into heaps of smoking ashes. (And sometimes those bombs are ones that we have built and delivered.)
All this we can now feel with a special intensity.

What follows from this kind of knowledge that we have
bought with so much grief? Should we try to close this window
of vulnerability? To do that would turn our country into a
prison. It would betray a heritage that we need to honor at all
costs, namely, that we live as a free people in a free land. And
we intend to keep it that way.

So we say to the world: We will try to learn from this bitter
lesson. There is no special status for the United States. We are,
together with all other peoples, guests on this planet, finite and
mortal beings who are connected to each other, dependent on
one another.

Therefore, we must regard our "American way of life," not
as a privilege to be defended at any cost against the rest of the
world, but rather, we must maintain it in such a way that it can
become a way of life for other peoples as well, if they so wish.

The way we see ourselves as a nation will have to be a way
compatible with the ways in which nature itself works. A way
that respects the variety of cultures and religions. A way to protect the rights of all peoples.

We are stunned by the hatred that reveals itself in these attacks. But we need to see the causes that enabled it to grow. We
need to find possibilities to decontaminate the conditions that
have contributed to the planning and execution of these heinous
crimes.

This implies the acknowledgment — and this may well be the
hardest task I ask of you today — that our vulnerability is also an
expression of our failure to meet peoples in other parts of the
world as the honest brokers for their needs. We need to accept
our share in the injustices that are causing so much suffering. The
evil is not simply out there; it is also with us and within us.

For a long time we have held onto our sense of national innocence. But it now lies buried under the rubble of the Twin
Towers in New York.

Why do I suggest this turn?

Not because we have suddenly become cowards, but because we have gained the insight that our security is linked to the security of all peoples. That our peace is connected to their peace. The freedom we cherish so much cannot be had without their freedom.

Many of you will say in anger that we have lost our nerve. That we are capitulating to the terrorists.

That is not the case.

America remains the most powerful nation of the world. But we are powerful enough to admit our vulnerability. We are sovereign enough to take this unprecedented turn. And thus we are not allowing the terrorists to dictate our response.

Does this mean that we let them get away with their crimes? By no means! They are murderers, and so they must be brought to an international court. We are calling on all the peoples around the globe, who so overwhelmingly share in our suffering, to assist us in identifying and prosecuting the assassins and their supporters. Since we have good reason to suspect that they are members of the Islamic religion, we are calling on Muslim lawyers to assist us. A fatwa by Muslim spiritual leaders would clarify that such crimes are incompatible with the spirit of Islam. Muslim experts could help us in setting up an International Court to which we will surely bring our claims and proofs.

Terrorism is one of the great plagues of our time. We do not pretend to be able to eradicate it, least of all by waging a war against it. Because evil — and terrorism is evil — will not disappear from the face of the earth because we wish it away. It will stay with us as a threat and a temptation because it is in all of us.

This is a bitter day. Let us turn it into a day of truth and honesty.

What I ask of you today is a burdensome task, certainly heaviest for the families whose loved ones have lost their lives. But I am convinced that this is the only way to liberate ourselves and others from the vicious cycle of violence and counterviolence.

God bless America!

Of course, an address such as this seems the remotest of possibilities. What we know about the spirituality of President Bush and, more importantly, about the self-understanding of most Americans, indeed of most human beings everywhere, suggests that such a text would stir up enormous disappointment and brooding anger.

Yet, even though this "draft" may sound absurdly unrealistic now, it was not entirely unthinkable in the immediate aftermath of the attacks. There was a good deal of self-questioning. Some U.S. citizens wanted to understand where so much hatred was coming from; and they did not believe in retaliation. Numerous experts pointed to the growing misery in African and Arab countries as one of the causes for the anger and frustration that facilitate terrorism. They argued that improving the desperate situation of so many human beings in disordered states with oppressive governments was altruistic, not only in the noblest tradition of the American people but also in the nation's best political and economic interests. As one of them (who prefers to be anonymous) said to me right after September 11: "The irony of the story is that empathy with the weak, hungry, and downtrodden that we know from churches, synagogues, and mosques would have to become the leading concept of U.S. realpolitik."

The sad fact, however, is that the administration in Washington did not give itself the necessary time to consider alternatives; nor did it allow the American people to think through the long-term effects of retaliation policies. Less than a week after 9/11, the "war on terrorism" was in the making. And not much more than a year after that, the Bush administration was advertising its inevitable invasion of Iraq to the American people as necessary because of Saddam Hussein's supposed ties with Al Qaeda and his supposed possession of weapons of mass destruction. As I write this (November 2005), an extension of this "war" to include Iran is improbable but not unthinkable. Global politics has come under the spell of terror and counterterror, while economic and social disparities spread, and the growing impacts of climate change go unattended.

It may appear utterly naive to suggest that vulnerability could be a key element in the politics of nations.[2] I will say more about this con-

2. I am aware of the fact that the term "vulnerability" is being criticized sharply by

cept in the following chapters. At this point I wish to emphasize that vulnerability is nothing to be abhorred; it is as inevitable and elementary as life itself. Only the dead are invulnerable (at least to human attacks). Together with all living things, we humans live on our ability to feel, to receive, and to share. Our vulnerability makes us susceptible to good and harmful impulses. It enables us to experience the heights and depths of love, as well as those of anger, hatred, and distrust. What we need most is what we fear most. As we acknowledge that vulnerability connects us with all other human beings — indeed, with all living creatures — it can become the guiding concept for our attempts to create systems of security. Vulnerability is the fundamental reference point for our understanding of human equality and justice: its basic claim is that every human being has the same right to receive health care, to live in safe conditions, to have access to education and jobs that provide decent living standards, to raise families, and to live and die with dignity. Accepting vulnerability as elementary for the human condition constitutes the foundation of human rights and of the integrity of all creation.

People who want to be invulnerable must make themselves impenetrable. Their search for invincibility must be paid for with the lifeless shield of numbed emotions and intellectual inertia. While suppressing their own insecurities and needs, they are forced to concentrate all their powers on fending off real and imagined enemies. This leads to false conceptions of the stranger, the other, and to a distorted sense of one's own identity. As a consequence, the avenues of communication

---

feminist thinkers. They regard the use of this concept as a more or less conscious, yet insidious "malestream" strategy to legitimate gender inequity. A telling example of this critique can be found in Sarah Coakley, *Powers and Submissions: Spirituality, Philosophy and Gender* (Oxford: Blackwell Publishers, 2002). Coakley does argue, however, that feminist philosophers and theologians need to work toward a more nuanced approach that is capable of taking into account the wide range of dependencies to which human life is subjected. Hence she does not really question the truth of the term "vulnerability"; she protests the overriding assumption that separates (female) vulnerability from (male) invulnerability and intends to transcend the illusionary though powerful dichotomy. This is exactly what I have in mind. In introducing a positive reading of vulnerability I want to establish it as a fundamental condition of the matrix of life in all of its forms on this planet.

and exchange are narrowed to dualistic perceptions of the problems and to confrontational methods of dealing with them.

What do these considerations have to do with 9/11? I will highlight two facets: one is that official America, as well as official Europe, failed to understand the symbolic message of the terrorist attacks; the second is that this failure has prevented the United States and its allies from recognizing the historical opportunity to exchange the predominant politics of retaliation for policies of reconciliation. Instead, the war on terrorism has further deepened the processes of dis-membership between Western nations and the so-called Arab world. It has also fueled the antagonisms between Israel and her Arab neighbors. And it has served as a justification for the Russian government's oppression of Chechnya. In addition, this dis-membership has divided the citizens of the United States in unprecedented ways, and it has widened the gap between European countries and the United States. Four years after 9/11, the world appears to be more insecure than before 9/11.

The Symbolic Message of the Attacks

It came as a shock to us all, everywhere in the world, how well organized international terrorism had become. Obviously, the attacks on the Twin Towers of the World Trade Center in New York and on the Pentagon, and the abortive attempt on the White House (it is likely that Flight 93, downed near Shanksville, Pennsylvania, was aimed at the White House) had been gruesomely well coordinated. These assaults were shocking not only in their murderous efficiency but also in their symbolic message.

I assume that the Twin Towers had no special symbolic meaning for most Americans; nor did Europeans regard them as particularly significant. Tourists in New York saw them as an interesting site; bankers and managers saw the towers as just one of the many administrative centers for an increasingly globalized economy. But for the millions of people in the so-called Third World, the Twin Towers symbolized an economic "world order" that brought them misery and deprivation, high mortality rates for their children, treks of refugees, exploitation, and humiliation.

Concerning the Pentagon, many in the United States and Europe see it as perhaps nothing more than a huge five-sided spider's web of military might. For millions of people in Latin America and the Caribbean, in Asia and in the Pacific, however, the Pentagon is the mighty fortress of the omnipresent, invincible superpower. For them it is the command center for the big and small wars, the open and covert operations by which the United States has exercised its might in ways that they can never forget. Whether in Cuba, Guatemala, or Nicaragua, in Panama, Colombia, or Chile — how much destruction, humiliation, and hatred have those interventions and "destabilization campaigns" caused? Similar images are true in Africa. And most recently, the omnipotence of the Pentagon has acquired a nightmarish presence in Arab countries. What causes so much anger is not just the insatiable thirst for oil, nor the Gulf Wars as such, nor its unconditional support for Israel. It is the additional humiliation, the experience of emasculation that cries out for revenge.

Most of our politicians in Europe and America have failed to recognize this underside of the history of confrontations between Western powers and Arab/Muslim countries. It dates back to the Crusades, and it is what I have identified above as the "hermeneutics of humiliation." It was intensified during the years of English and French colonialist control; and it has deepened in recent times because of the United States' open support, for example, of corrupt governments in Arab regions and the shaming presence of U.S. military personnel on or near the holy sites of Islam. This history of humiliation has diminished the sense of honor and pride in many Muslim men and women.

And now, behold, the Twin Towers had fallen! The Pentagon, that impenetrable fortress, showed a big gash. To be sure, people around the world mourned for the innocent women and men who had lost their lives in the explosion, sympathizing with them and their families because they know what it means to be so vulnerably exposed to bombings and massacres. Yet, at the same time, many of these women and men felt a hidden and grim satisfaction. For once the mighty Americans, the condescending "gringos," had suffered what they had been through so often. What they felt can be summed up in a harsh statement: the attacks hit individual people who were innocent, but they also hit a nation that is not innocent in its use of power.

From the perspective of those who have been humiliated by the West — and especially by the United States — those attacks on the Pentagon and the Twin Towers were not a declaration of war and thus the beginning of a "new era"; the attacks were nothing other than the continuation of the everyday war of which they had been the victims for so long. In their view, the "low intensity warfare" that had destabilized their lives had simply come back to the place where it had originated. Time and again, the United States had sent out their Marines and exported their wars. Now, for the first time — and for the entire world to see on television — this murderous violence had returned to the centers of America's might.

Such a perception of the crimes of 9/11 is shocking to people in Europe, and much more so to citizens of the United States. Such grim satisfaction appears to be nothing but an odious *Schadenfreude* that should be forbidden in the face of the three thousand human beings who were killed. And yet there is a painful reason for such grim resentment, and the political leaders in the powerful nations should have been wise enough to consider it. It is often said that there is a cry for help in every suicide. What kind of cry was there in the suicide attacks of 9/11? This is an awesome question that is almost too sinister to mention. But it might have been wise to listen to such a silent cry.

Most political leaders in Europe did not wish to see this symbolism; they only had eyes for a different symbolic dimension of the terrorist attacks. When German Chancellor Schroeder, speaking for the majority of Germans, talked about a "declaration of war against the entire civilized world," he voiced only disgust and horror. The political leaders of other nations voiced their protest in similar ways. But what exactly was this "declaration of war," and what did the chancellor mean when he spoke of the "civilized world"?

He meant the deep horror that civilized women and men feel when they are faced with other human beings who are ready to kill themselves as a means to kill others. That goes against our understanding of the sanctity of life. There is a firm agreement among all civilized people that innocent human beings must not be sacrificed for any means, least of all for inhuman fanatical ends. Another aspect that provokes disgust and horror is the fact that entire airplanes, together with their crews and passengers, had been turned into gigantic bombs. Our civilization depends on a reliable mobility, for which airplanes are gleaming symbols of dependability and control. Those who travel on airplanes need to be confident that they will be brought to their desired destination, not to their death.

The atrocity of the attacks, however, should not have concealed from the eyes of our political leaders the sad fact that our "civilized" world is uncivilized — brutal and inhuman — for the majority of the world's peoples. The reactions to 9/11 in the West manifested a systemic blindness. We in Europe and in America do not wish to admit that we bear the primary responsibility for the economic and social destabilizations that leave large parts of humankind in misery and wide regions of the earth in environmental degradation. The United States — and, to a lesser degree, the European states — are accountable for the fact that dictators, warlords, and clan chieftains, including Arab ones, can get their hands on all the weapons they can pay for. Without those weapons they would not be able to lead the murderous civil wars in which even children are deadly fighters.

Who provided the Taliban with weapons? Who helped to set up Saddam Hussein in the first place? And who provided assistance for Saddam's war against Iran? Who stands by as the Muslim government of Sudan terrorizes the mostly Christian people in the south or the black Muslims in the Darfur region? Which country is not willing to sign the treaty to ban landmines?

So we must face this question: How do these attitudes relate to the much-talked-about civility and rule of law in the free world? The acts of 9/11 left no time for self-critical questions such as these. There was genuine mourning around the globe; and there was a great willingness to help. But the profound sadness within the United States was soon absorbed by self-righteous anger. American flags fluttered wherever one looked. The question, "Why do they hate us?" was asked around the country; but too often it was accompanied by the ominous query, "How can we punish anyone who does?" The delicately nuanced answers that needed articulation were drowned out by the millennial thunder of "The Battle Hymn of the Republic," repeatedly sung at 9/11 commemorations. And the singing of "God Bless America" at baseball stadiums around the country, begun in New York after 9/11 to commemorate those policemen and firemen who had perished, is now a staple at the beginning of baseball games; it is sung along with the national anthem in yet another expression of American civil religion.

The furious haste with which President Bush rallied the nation for the "war on terrorism" manifests the resurgence of America's messianic sense of mission. No time was spent to reflect on whether this experience of vulnerability might yield a positive message. America's wounded heart cried out for revenge — and got it.

This response to the terrorist attacks accounts for the rapid erosion of worldwide support for the U.S. rush to war. Only one year after 9/11, there were mass demonstrations all over the world against the plans of the Bush administration to go to war against Iraq. This widespread distrust of America is one of the sad "new" things that 9/11 has brought about.

Ground Zero in New York

The published pictures of Ground Zero in New York are countless. For months the forlorn remains of the Twin Towers' concrete skeleton reached up into the skies. From everywhere women and men traveled to New York, among them many politicians, to pay tribute to all those who mourned at this site. In many families and churches — including my own church — people prayed for the bereaved families and collected money for them. For weeks the *New York Times* reported on each of the victims and tried to reconstruct their stories and the circumstances of their death.

Now, some five years later, there is still the open wound between the surrounding high-rise buildings, which has been named "Ground Zero." But plans for a new tower are in place, and it will be higher and more spectacular than the Twin Towers ever were. The design by architect Libeskind will leave an open space for Ground Zero, a space of memorial to those who perished there on September 11, 2001.

What will be remembered? What will the function and purpose of that memorial be? Will it be a place of mourning or a stage for nurturing anger? Will it provide the space needed not only to remember the death of three thousand human beings but also the horrible deaths of other human beings in other places of pain? Furthermore, will there be, for example, a memorial to the 16,000 human beings of Bhopal, India, who died when a poisonous gas explosion occurred in a plant owned by the American firm Union Carbide? Or again, will there be space to remember the destruction wreaked by the rockets President Clinton unleashed against the pharmaceutical plant of Al-Shifa in Sudan in August 1998?[3]

To put the question another way, will the way September 11 is remembered in the United States lead to a strengthening of compassion for the many forms of suffering human beings endure around the world? Will it be inclusive enough to embrace the pain of victims in other places? Or will it be exclusive, reserved for America's victims only? As the matter currently stands, it appears that the latter option has preference. It looks as though the attack on the Twin Towers will be regarded as a singular crime that cannot be compared to any other crimes. This kind of exclusive remembering will change the 9/11 memorial into a shrine of America's hurt, destined to stoke the fires of revenge. If it goes in that direction, Ground Zero in Manhattan will foster selective memory and prolong the hermeneutics of denial that has followed America's messianic project like a sinister shadow.

Let us take a closer look. "Ground zero" originated as a technical military term that identified the point at which a bomb inflicts its gravest damage. It acquired a special meaning in locating the radius of destruction for atomic bombs, which is why the term became part of popular use when two atomic bombs were dropped on the Japanese

3. James Risen, "To Bomb Sudan Plants, Or Not: A Year Later, Debates Rankle," *New York Times*, Oct. 27, 1999, p. A1. Because the strike damaged a plant that produced antimalarial drugs in an impoverished region, Werner Daum, former German ambassador to the Sudan, saw elements of state terrorism in the attack. See http://en.wikipedia.org/wiki/Werner_Daum.

cities of Hiroshima and Nagasaki in August 1945. That is the original cultural context of "ground zero." Thus it is quite revealing to compare the vastly different ways in which these two ground zeroes are being remembered.

In chapter 4, I mentioned the story of the Smithsonian Institute's attempt to create an exhibit on the occasion of the fiftieth anniversary of the bombing of Hiroshima and Nagasaki. There was adamant resistance, most notably from groups of veterans. Their argument was that the exhibit was pro-Japanese and that it would dishonor U.S. servicemen. The columnist George Will wrote that the curators of the Smithsonian were "un-American." Both houses of Congress passed resolutions condemning the exhibit.[4] After many disputes, the Institute decided to give it up altogether. The only things remaining on display were the *Enola Gay,* a plaque, and a tape of the flight crew. The target cities, Hiroshima and Nagasaki, with all their dead human beings, were not mentioned at all. In fact, it was demanded that no signs of Japanese suffering be displayed within the exhibit.

There is a connection between the plan of the Smithsonian Institute in 1995 and the Ground Zero memorial in New York. Both are examples of selective remembering that are dictated by zealous patriotism and the belief in superheroic innocence.

Ground Zero in Dresden

Many Americans may feel that this is the only adequate reaction to a heinous attack such as 9/11. However, from my German experience, I wish to argue the possibility of quite different reactions by telling the story of the *Frauenkirche* ("Our Lady's Church") in the city of Dresden. On October 30, 2005, this famous baroque church — it had often been called the most beautiful Protestant church in Germany — was reconsecrated as a "place of remembrance" and a "center of reconciliation." It is a forceful reminder of another "ground zero," which

4. Robert J. Lifton and Greg Mitchell, *Hiroshima in America: Fifty Years of Denial* (New York: G. P. Putnam, 1995), p. xii.

occurred on February 13, 1945, when British and U.S. bombers attacked Dresden on the Elbe River, a city famous for its architectural beauties and artistic treasures. The bombing raids created a devastating firestorm. Many tens of thousands of children, men, and women perished; as a matter of fact, nobody will ever know the exact number of fatalities because the city was overflowing with refugees. (Some estimates speak of 200,000 victims, but this number seems exaggerated.) The center of the ancient city, acclaimed as the "Florence on the Elbe River," lay in ruins. In the middle of it, the *Frauenkirche* stood burning for two days; then it, too, collapsed in a heap of rubble.

It remained so for some decades. The communist leaders of the former Democratic Republic had no intention — even if the necessary means had been available — to reconstruct this magnificent church. More than twenty-five years ago I stood in front of the ruins: birch trees had grown in the rubble, their branches reaching out through the gaping holes that had once been windows. In 1982, young pacifist women and men of Dresden began to place candles at the site of the ruins. In the following years the site became a place of remembering and a focus of the peace movement, which was under constant harassment by the communist government and its agencies. Then, in 1990, after the fall of the Berlin Wall, a group of citizens launched an appeal for the reconstruction of the *Frauenkirche*. It met with overwhelming success; people from all over the world contributed to it. Four years later, the extremely difficult process of rebuilding began, and now the magnificent church is back in place.

More magnificent than the structure itself are the stories of reconciliation that occurred in this rebuilding process. I will mention just two. For many years, the Christians of Dresden and those of the English city of Coventry had established close contacts. Coventry had been heavily attacked by German bombers in 1941. German youth groups helped to construct the new cathedral that has been erected next to the ruins of the medieval one. Dresden churches joined the "Cross of Nails Community," which originated in Coventry as a network of reconciliation. Then the "Dresden Trust," under the leadership of Dr. Allan Russell (with the Duke of Kent taking his patronage very seriously), became active and raised over 750,000 British pounds

— of which a large part was dedicated to the construction of a nine-meter-tall orb and cross. (Incidentally, the man who did most of the work on this magnificent cross, using the original eighteenth-century techniques as much as possible, is Alan Smith, son of one of the pilots involved in the raid on Dresden.)[5]

Then there is the story of people in the Polish town of Gostyn. Back in 1942, an underground guerrilla group of mostly young men from Gostyn were captured. Twelve of them were executed in one of Dresden's public squares; those who were not shot because they were under sixteen years of age survived in concentration camps. After the war, some of them returned to Dresden to look after the graves of their comrades. In this way contacts between churches in Gostyn and Dresden began to form. And so the Polish visitors learned of the suffering that had befallen their old enemies. When they heard of the plans for rebuilding the *Frauenkirche,* they decided to contribute to it. The city council of Gostyn dedicated money to help with the carving of a special stone in the shape of a flame, which was then integrated into the building as a token of reconciliation between Poles and Germans.

With church attendance being what it is in Germany, Dresden did not need an additional church. But the *Frauenkirche* has a special mission, which goes far beyond the city limits and even beyond the borders of Germany: it is a mission of reconciliation, and it is based on deep remembering. The church has already become a place to be visited not only by tourists but by school classes and youth groups of all kinds. There they learn about the past, the guilt and the suffering, and there they get a glimpse of what reconciliation and common commitment can do to create new and beautiful things. In its programs the *Frauenkirche* aims to speak to people from all over Europe — and beyond — about the possibility of turning places of shame and hurt into places of joy and hope.

---

5. For details on the history of the *Frauenkirche* and its programs, see the Web display: www.frauenkirche-dresden.org (accessed Dec. 20, 2005).

Ground Zero and Cultures of Remembering

The *Frauenkirche* can be seen as a symbolic expression of a culture of deep remembering that marks European history after World War II. The long-term impact of that "Second Great European War" is clearly distinguishable from that of World War I. While the Versailles Treaty of 1919 was dictated by what I call a "politics of retaliation," the lessons drawn from the devastations of the 1939-1945 war have been informed by more integrative methods (which did not, as I have indicated, exclude the question of guilt). The founding generation of political leaders working for the European Community in the decade following that terrible catastrophe, such as Robert Schumann, Konrad Adenauer, and others, had come out of the horrors of the European onslaught with the firm conviction that the old enmities needed to be overcome by something that resembled a politics of reconciliation.

To be sure, many of today's political leaders no longer share this deep commitment to reconciliation. For them the European Community appears to be a platform of economic interests only. Thus there is ample need within Europe to keep alive a wider and more substantial vision: the European Community as a region of peace. Europe is full of "ground zeroes"; it is a continent replete with stories of vain victories and unspeakable sufferings. The deaths of millions of human beings, the streams of refugees, the destruction of so many cities — all these things are alive in our collective memory. Although everyone agrees that Hitler had to be fought until the end, there is little comfort in those victories for the Russians, the British, the French — at least for the people at the grass-roots level. The prices they have had to pay have been terribly high.

In the United States, most people still tend to think that going to war means that a resounding victory will follow; in Europe, most people tend to think that nothing can be won by going to war. This is the point at which one can observe a profound difference in the cultures of remembering between Europeans and Americans. People on this side of the Atlantic are slowly coming to understand that denial does not help them. Truth about the past and empathy with those who bore the burdens are part of the process of healing the wounds of separation and distrust. I am not saying that the growth of the peoples of Europe toward a sustainable community has been completed. There will always be new challenges and stumbling blocks, from within and from without; the relationships with the African nations and those in the Middle East may prove to be the most important. Yet, despite all these reservations, I am convinced that the European Community is a historic and even unprecedented experiment in reconciliation politics.[6]

There is certainly no reason to be triumphalistic about this process. A grave reminder of the indecisiveness and rivalry among European nations became visible in the way they mishandled the civil wars among the Balkan peoples after the disintegration of Yugoslavia. Another example of disunity was the approach of European countries to the war against Iraq. Some chose to enter the U.S.-led "coalition forces," while others, notably France and Germany, decided not to be (directly) involved. Much work remains to be done, and it may well be that the Europeans and their political leaders will not live up to the lessons their history has offered to teach them.

There are American observers who dismiss the relevance of what I have just said by arguing that the Europeans have only been able to pursue their happy social and pacifist maneuvers because the mighty American eagle has protected them from the evils of the world. Michael Hirsh, for instance, is bold enough to declare:

> Set aside for a moment the precipitous invasions of Iraq. America spends more on defense than the rest of the industrialized world combined not because it is inherently belligerent or militaristic but mainly because America is today more than just the "lone superpower." It is the stabilizer of the international system. American power overlays every region of the planet, and it supplies the control rods that restrain belligerents and arms races from East Asia to Latin America, enabling globalization to proceed apace. . . . Yet, for too many post–cold War Europeans, this stabilizing structure of American power has been so hidden

6. See Hans Eckehard Bahr, *Erbarmen mit Amerika: Deutsche Alternativen* (Berlin: Aufbau-Verlag, 2005), esp. pp. 84ff.

as not to be worthy of note. Why exactly do they think their governments can afford to spend so little on defense (thereby subsidizing the European welfare state)? As with the children in Anna Karenina, "there is no need for us to think about that, it's all ready for us."[7]

There is a lot that is sorely wrong with such a statement. The most cynical aspect of Hirsh's reasoning is that he describes the commitments to welfare states in Europe as a kind of child's play made possible by the big father in Washington, who is altruistic enough to do the bloody work. (Does Hirsh not know that the building up of these "welfare state systems" has been a very costly process indeed, taking the lives of thousands of trade unionists and laborers, and going back to the second half of the nineteenth century, that is, long before the rise of the United States to its superpower status?) If one were to take Hirsh's argument to its logical conclusion, the African-Americans of New Orleans owe their misery to us Europeans because Washington needs to (indirectly) subsidize our lavish "socialist" plays — so there's no money left to look after the poor within the borders of the United States.

The point is that, due to their many ground zero experiences, European nations have learned the lesson that the functioning integrity of societies is as much dependent on social stability and just labor relations as it is on their military establishments. For the United States, on the other hand, the experience of being the global winner has become a trap. President Eisenhower's prophetic warning about the danger of the "military-industrial complex" tending to become the all-encompassing economic factor has become all too true.[8] Sadly, Hirsh is correct when he admits that the United States is spending more money on the military buildup than all the industrialized nations combined. But the reason he offers is wrong: his idea that this is a historic necessity to "keep globalization apace" is a piece of propaganda that

7. Michael Hirsh, "Bloody Necessary," *Washington Monthly,* April 2005: www.washingtonmonthly.com/features/2005/0504.hirsh.html (accessed Nov. 20, 2005).

8. Dwight D. Eisenhower, "Military Industrial Complex Speech, 1961" (The Avalon Project at Yale University: http://www.yale.edu/lawweb/avalon/presiden/speeches/eisenhower001.htm [accessed Dec. 18, 2005]).

carries America's redeemer nation image to its militaristic extreme. It is not possible, as Hirsh suggests, to "set aside for a moment the precipitous invasions of Iraq," as if they were a kind of minor "mistake" to be discarded in the formulation of the grand equation. They are part and parcel of the global conquest for the American empire. What would hinder any outsider from thinking that these invasions are stark examples of the U.S. military-industrial complex feeding on itself? "The only arms race is one that we are having with ourselves," says former President Jimmy Carter.[9]

In his book *America Right or Wrong,* the British correspondent and researcher Anatol Lieven raises the question of "why a country which after the terrorist attacks of September 11, 2001, had the chance to create a concert of all the world's major states — including Muslim ones — against Islamist revolutionary terrorism chose instead to pursue policies which divided the West, further alienated the Muslim world and exposed America itself to greatly increased dangers."[10] Such a question needs a nuanced response. One contribution to an answer lies in the issue I have discussed in this chapter: How can we deal with vulnerability? What is the relationship between experiences of vulnerability and cultures of remembering and the political-military options derived from them? As Lieven implies (and as my "presidential speech draft" at the beginning of this chapter would argue), 9/11 provided the United States with the opportunity to create a new and comprehensive global "concert" against terrorism. It missed the opportunity. The West is divided, and we can now observe new levels of anti-Europeanism and anti-Americanism. The alienation of predominantly Muslim countries has reached new intensity. And the United States, in its quest for invulnerability, has become more insecure than it ever was before.

It will not suffice to put the blame on President Bush and his administration alone. The temptation is there, and it will increase as the Iraqi quagmire continues to get worse. But this would be a sort of

9. Jimmy Carter, *Our Endangered Values: America's Moral Crisis* (New York: Simon & Schuster, 2005), p. 199.

10. Quoted by M. Hirsh, "Bloody Necessary," p. 2; Anatol Lieven, *America Right or Wrong: An Anatomy of American Nationalism* (New York: Oxford University Press, 2004).

scapegoating, and it would prevent us from looking at the underlying issues. Former President Carter has suggested that, during the past twenty-five years, U.S. administrations have initiated policies that are in contradiction to previously held principles. He attributes this "moral crisis" to a "fundamentalism" that merges religious and political ideas.[11] As a remedy, he suggests:

> Our government should be known, without question, as opposed to war, dedicated to the resolution of disputes by peaceful means. . . . We should be seen as the unswerving champion of freedom and human rights, both among our own citizens and within the global community. America should be the focal point around which other nations of all kinds could marshal to combat threats to security and to enhance the quality of our common environment.[12]

Carter seems to think that the fundamentalist revolution now reigning in Washington can be overcome by simply returning to the ideals of the past, which he describes as follows:

> Americans have always been justifiably proud of our country, beginning with our forefathers' bold Declaration of Independence and their pronouncement "that all men are created equal, that they are endowed by their Creator with certain unalienable Rights, that among these are Life, Liberty and the pursuit of Happiness." Since then, our people have utilized America's great natural resources, access to warm oceans, relatively friendly neighbors, a heterogeneous population, and a pioneering spirit to form a "more perfect union."[13]

This, however, is a more than idyllic description of America's history. Valuable though his self-criticism is, Carter himself engages in se-

---

11. Carter, *Endangered Values*, pp. 30ff., 94ff.
12. Carter, *Endangered Values*, pp. 199f.
13. Carter, *Endangered Values*, p. 198.

lective remembering. He idealizes the American conquest (I wonder what the "relatively friendly neighbors" of whom Carter speaks would say to this!). There is no mention of the violence implied in this "pursuit," no dealing with the inherent guilt and the massive hatred that has accumulated around the world in response to it.

So Carter's remedy will not work. The moral crisis that he diagnoses goes deeper, and it is this idealistic self-image itself that is part of the crisis. Deep remembering would have to take a more profound — and more painful — look at the flipside of America's rise to power. Many people around the world are waiting for American political leaders great enough to admit the misdeeds of the United States and courageous enough to redefine its role among the nations of the world. The acknowledgment of vulnerability that the people of the United States share with all the peoples around the globe would prove to be a more honest and creative way forward than the illusionary pursuit of invulnerability. Could there be a lesson in the ways Europe has emerged from the horrors of World War II that citizens of the United States may wish to study?

CHAPTER 6

Clash of Fundamentalisms

―≈―

D id Samuel Huntington's best-selling book *The Clash of Civiliza-tions* promote what it had hoped to prevent?[1] Huntington had picked up "the clash of civilizations" phrase from Bernard Lewis, who had also issued a warning about dealing with "the roots of Muslim rage," which he saw in the incendiary incidents when pilgrims to Mecca were killed, in the bombing of the U.S. embassy in Pakistan, and in the fatwas issued against Salman Rushdie after his book *The Satanic Verses* was published. In the words of Lewis:

> This is no less than a clash of civilizations — the perhaps irra-tional but surely historic reaction of an ancient rival against our Judeo-Christian heritage, our secular present, and the world-wide expansion of both. It is crucially important that we on our side should not be provoked into an equally historic but also equally irrational reaction against that rival.[2]

1. Samuel Huntington, "The Clash of Civilizations," *Foreign Affairs* 72, no. 3 (1993): 22ff. This article was extended into a book entitled *The Clash of Civilizations and the Remaking of World Order* (New York: Simon & Schuster, 1996).
2. Bernard Lewis, "The Roots of Muslim Rage," *The Atlantic Monthly*, September 1990.

Huntington wanted his title to reaffirm the possibility of such dangerous developments in the future, and thus wished to warn Western nations not to become involved in them. Instead, his book has been taken as a factual description of an inevitable direction for global civilizations. The attacks of September 11, 2001, seemed to prove that Huntington's prophecies had come true. And Lewis himself apparently became a kind of guru to the neoconservatives in Washington, who aimed to convert Iraq into another nation on the model of Turkey.[3] With the rise of religiously motivated international terrorism, a superficially grasped "clash-theory" has seemed an easy blueprint on which political leaders can base their confrontational strategies. Those who take the trouble to read Huntington's work, however, will soon learn that his arrangement of the world's civilizations — their fault lines and possible antagonistic trends — is far too general and superficial to provide the succinct scheme it pretends to offer.

In fact, if one takes a more careful look at the civilizations of the earth, one discovers that they are not necessarily "clash"-committed but flexible enough to allow for a wide variety of openness, interconnectedness, and mutuality. The political, economic, technological, cultural, and religious elements of globalization indicate to varying degrees that there is a great deal of exchange and cooperation. Scientists, musicians, engineers, and businesspeople move freely among and between cultures and civilizations. Some observers speak of an "intercultural humanism" that constitutes a substantial bond between people of different worldviews and convictions.[4] A powerful example of this boundary-transcending humanism is offered in the life vocation of Mahatma Gandhi: he was a strong Hindu, but his perspective encompassed basic elements of Christianity, and he went out of his way to befriend Muslims. His nonviolent methods of approaching political conflicts became widely known and eventually informed people of the

3. See Michael Hirsh, "Bernard Lewis Revisited," *Washington Monthly*, November 2004: http://www.washingtonmonthly.com/features/2004/0411.hirsh.html (accessed Jan. 16, 2006).

4. See Ram Adhar Mall and Klaudius Gansczyk, "Interkultureller Humanismus als Hoffnung für das 21. Jahrhundert," *Hoffnung Europa: Strategie des Miteinander* (Hamburg: Global Marshall Plan Initiative, 2006), pp. 63-79.

most diverse civilizations. The South African struggle against apartheid owes much to Gandhi, as does the civil rights movement in the United States.

Lewis's and Huntington's "clash" slogan appears to be true with regard to the so-called Muslim world. But here, too, the approach is far too general to be of much help. We should not forget, for example, that the Ottoman Empire, until its demise in 1919, was far more tolerant with regard to religious minorities than were the Christian realms of its time. Even today, if one looks at conditions in Malaysia, Indonesia, Iran, or Morocco, one cannot help recognizing the enormous pluralism within these predominantly Muslim countries. As a matter of fact, it makes more sense to understand the world's civilizations as distinctive, yet at the same time exhibiting widely overlapping networks of meaning that display more commonalities than elements of confrontation (about which I will say more at the end of this chapter). The question here is: How did the warning that was implicit in the "clash of civilizations" phrase get lost and become instead a call to confrontation? One kind of answer comes from Tariq Ali's book *The Clash of Fundamentalisms* (2002), which he wrote as a deliberate and provocative correction of the Lewis-Huntington phrase and concept.[5] Ali's basic argument is that civilizations and religious systems become "clash-prone" whenever they are "kidnapped" by fundamentalisms. His own vision of the dangers of fundamentalism arises out of an experience that no one else would wish to have.

Tariq Ali was born in 1943 into a feudal family whose home was Lahore — at that time in India, now in Pakistan. At the time of Ali's birth, that famous city was under British colonial rule, and its population consisted mainly of Muslims, Sikhs, and Hindus. Ali's family was Muslim, but only in a very superficial way. In fact, they thought of the mullahs as rather silly, despicable men of no standing in their society — and certainly people of no political importance. However, the multicultural accommodations in Lahore disintegrated in the unspeakable horrors that erupted in 1947, when Pakistan and India were partitioned into

5. Tariq Ali, *The Clash of Fundamentalisms: Crusades, Jihads and Modernity* (London, New York: Verso, 2002).

separate countries. Millions of Muslims were killed or forced to flee to the new nation of Pakistan, while millions of Hindus and Sikhs were murdered or forced to move away from what had become Pakistani territory. Tariq Ali's father, in disgust, distanced himself from this religiously motivated turmoil and became an orthodox communist; his son followed him into this secular, even atheistic, tradition.

But September 11, 2001, changed his perspective on religious identities. Tariq Ali, who now lives in London after his Oxford education — a non-Muslim agnostic with Muslim roots — felt that he was compelled to study in earnest what had happened to the Muslims and what had changed their worldviews in such dramatic ways. Why did Wahhabism become so prevalent in Saudi Arabia? What made people enthusiastic about the Arab League? What compelled so many people to join the Muslim Brotherhood? How can one understand the ardent anticolonialism of the Middle East? Why do India and Pakistan both think that they need atomic bombs to keep the other at bay?

Ali's book shows that there is a long story behind the catastrophe of September 11, 2001. If we want to find a path to a future without such grievous assaults, we must study and understand the suicide attacks. In Ali's words:

> We have to understand the despair, but also the lethal exaltation, that drives people to sacrifice their own lives. If Western politicians remain ignorant of the causes and carry on as before, there will be repetitions. Moral outrage has some therapeutic value, but as a political strategy it is useless. Lightly disguised wars of revenge waged in the heat of the moment are not much better. To fight tyranny and oppression by using tyrannical and oppressive means . . . will not further the cause of justice or bring about a meaningful democracy. It can only prolong the cycle of violence.[6]

Ali wrote these words in 2002. Since that time, the "war against terrorism," not only the second war against Iraq but also the building of the

6. Ali, *Clash of Fundamentalisms*, p. 3.

wall between Israeli and Palestinian territories, have given Tariq Ali's warning a gruesome truth. The cycle of violence has become fiercer than it was before. The unwillingness — or inability — to understand the root causes reveals a growing fundamentalism. So what we are seeing today is a clash of fundamentalisms.

Tariq Ali insists that Islamic fundamentalism cannot be properly understood without recognizing its corresponding manifestations in the West. For him, United States imperialism provides the oppressive context against which Muslim fundamentalists try to fight. He sees "globalization" as a term to camouflage the global hegemony of the United States. To substantiate this point, he quotes Thomas L. Friedman, the world-renowned columnist of the *New York Times,* who wrote in 1999:

> For globalization to work, America can't be afraid to act like the almighty superpower that it is. The hidden hand of the market will never work without a hidden fist. McDonald's cannot flourish without McDonnell-Douglas, the designer of the F-15, and the hidden fist that keeps the world safe for Silicon Valley's technology is called the United States Army, Air Force, Navy and Marine Corps.[7]

In Tariq Ali's view, the "clash of fundamentalisms" appears to be nothing but the confrontation between the hegemonic arrogance of the United States, on the one hand, and the many religiously camouflaged and suicidal, yet impotent, attacks and rebellions from the Muslim side. But there is more to fundamentalism, and to its inherent violence, than this assertion of superpower and the raging response to it.

7. Thomas L. Friedman, *New York Times,* March 28, 1999, quoted by Tariq Ali, *Clash of Fundamentalisms,* pp. 260f. For a fuller exposition of United States' triumphalism, see Thomas L. Friedman, *The Lexus and the Olive Tree* (New York: Farrar, Straus & Giroux, 1999), where he repeats the same statement on p. 373.

The Pains of Modernity

"Fundamentalism" is a term that should be used with caution. Although it has legitimate descriptive uses, it has become a denunciatory term that is often used to mark opponents as fanatical and irrational enemies. Although there is no way to describe an "essence of fundamentalism" that satisfies everyone, one can talk about some recurring patterns of belief and behavior. How, and under what conditions, did fundamentalism originate? As a starting point, I pose a very simple observation: as human beings we all need fundamentals. And we need the place and the time to appropriate them consciously. But what are "fundamentals"? Consider these at least: the nurturing love and sustaining care of our families and homes, the reliable and steadfast relationships of local communities and religious groups, the reliable networks of legal order, of customs, values and cultural traditions. These are the systems of meaning or, in George Lakoff's term, the "frames" that provide human beings with the means to discover their own strengths and to develop a role in life.[8] Hence human life unfolds by way of appropriating and transforming the legacies of our past. Each of us is more than a simple copy of our ancestors, though we remain indebted to them in more ways than we know or wish to admit. Our vitality and the vitality of our cultures and civilizations depend on how we are able to reconstruct the traditional systems of meaning and to "reframe" the inherited frames while at the same time responding energetically to the challenges of tomorrow. Hence we exist in the tension between the energies that tie us to our past and the energies that beckon us toward the future. So we need fundamentals. And we need fundamental trust, or "primordial trust," as Erik Erikson called it, in order to lead meaningful lives.

What kinds of circumstances lead this constant process of appropriating our fundamentals toward fundamentalism? This occurs in all those situations where the processes of appropriation are breaking down. Whenever the stabilizing systems of meaning and cultural frames dissolve, people will reach for fundamentalist solutions. (Or

8. Lakoff developed the "frames of meaning" concept most recently in *Don't Think of an Elephant* (White River Junction, VT: Chelsea Green Publishing, 2004).

they will give up any search for meaning and adopt "protean" life-styles, which I discuss later in this chapter.) These fundamentalist "solutions" comprise essentially three components: (1) the absolutizing of sacred texts and/or traditions; (2) orthodoxy, that is, the unquestioning observance of an absolute set of foundational beliefs; and (3) orthopraxy, that is, the equally unfailing observance of an absolute set of moral values. This is a drastic attempt to re-establish a meaningful world amid circumstances that appear to be chaotic.

When we examine these broad patterns in fundamentalism, we can see that we are faced with fundamentalist reactions all over the world, especially in situations of grave social disorder and prolonged civil wars, with their associated pressures of misery, uprootedness, and homelessness. These are the conditions that cause people to reframe their lives and worldviews around a few truths that offer the feeling of absolute security. What I am suggesting here is a cultural-anthropological and psycho-social perspective that can help explain not only the rapid growth of fundamentalisms around the world but also their "necessity" as symptoms of the legitimate quest for meaning. They are, in short, *pathological reactions* to living conditions that are too dislocating and destructive for people to bear. It seems apparent, then, that the global spread of modernity, including its overpowering economic pressure and pervasive cultural impact, is a force that provokes an upsurge of fundamentalist reactions.

Karen Armstrong investigates the spread of modernity in her impressive book *The Battle for God*.[9] For her, the history of modernity begins with 1492, the year that marks the "discovery" of the New World and the expulsion of the Jews from Spain. It is a history with two faces. One strand of it tells of dazzling conquests, groundbreaking discoveries, and revolutions that open up unprecedented opportunities to humankind. But it is the same historical period that presents us with a history of enslavement and genocidal crimes, of profound anxieties, and of frustrating disappointments.

9. Armstrong, *The Battle for God* (New York: Ballantine, 2001). See also Klaus Kienzler, *Der religiöse Fundamentalismus: Christentum, Judentum, Islam* (München: Büchergilde Lizenzausgabe, Beck'sche Verlagsbuchhandlung, 1996).

Fundamentalism is a reaction to the violent underside of modernity. The more acceleration we see, for instance, in technological and economic matters, or the more complexities we observe, for instance, in the world of politics and science, the greater the temptation to strictly reduce this confusion by settling for a few safe and irrefutable beliefs. This *reductionism* is a basic characteristic of every fundamentalist system.

The term "fundamentalism" was coined in 1920 in the United States by Baptist editor Curtis Lee Laws, who pledged that the faithful would "do battle royal for the Fundamentals." During the preceding decade there had been an influential series of articles by one hundred writers, from many religious denominations, that concentrated on key elements of the Christian faith, entitled *The Fundamentals: A Testimony to the Truth*.[10] These writers represented a strong movement among conservative and evangelical Protestants that rejected the spread of historical-critical interpretations of the Bible. They considered the new ways of interpreting the Bible a betrayal of the eternal truth of Holy Scripture. At the same time, these early "fundamentalists" were reacting firmly and negatively to the increasing liberal, communist, and otherwise "ungodly" trends in the sprawling American society. The term "fundamentalism" promised to provide a safe ground for Bible-believing men and women of steadfast faith and moral strength, people who were committed to stand firm against the decadent tendencies of the modern age.

Opposed by liberal Protestant ministers such as Harry Emerson Fosdick, who favored tolerance over certainty,[11] Protestant fundamentalism kept a fairly low political profile for more than half a century. The so-called Scopes Monkey Trial of 1925 was an event-focused outburst that had no discernible effect on political parties. But with the rise of the "Moral Majority" in the mid-1970s, under the leadership of Jerry Falwell, it became a political force, and it has managed to consolidate its power base in many communities, notably within the Republi-

10. Mark A. Noll, *A History of Christianity in the United States* (Grand Rapids: Eerdmans, 1992), pp. 381-82.
11. Noll, *History*, pp. 383-84.

can party.[12] We should note that this fundamentalist movement is by no means homogeneous. In fact, while the more radical branches have accepted dispensationalist end-time scenarios, combined with a strong patriotic nationalism (as I have discussed in chapter 2), there are other communities that prefer to call themselves "fundamental" purely in the sense of orthodox, conservative Christianity.[13]

Therefore, we cannot take fundamentalism to describe the whole broad spectrum of conservative Protestantism. In fact, we must bear in mind that fundamentalism is not only a descriptive term but one that typically encompasses evaluative and judgmental notions that differ according to one's own stance. Hence what looks "fundamentalist" from a liberal perspective may well be regarded as "liberal" from the other end of the spectrum.[14] We should also add that fundamentalism is by no means solely a creation of twentieth-century Protestantism. A similar process took place within the Roman Catholic Church during the same period: most important in this respect was the "anti-modernism oath" that Pope Pius X introduced in 1907.[15] The entire Catholic clergy had to swear that they would strictly adhere to the teachings of the official church and the fundamental aspects of its doctrine. This oath was not repealed until 1967, and even then its repeal did not terminate the powers of the Holy See to silence unorthodox positions and punish those who held them.[16]

12. Noll, *History,* pp. 445-46.

13. As an example, see the editorial "Fundamentalist or Fundamental?" Brethren Revival Fellowship, *BRF Witness,* vol. 28, no. 6 (Nov./Dec. 1993): www.brfwitness.org/Articles/1993v28n6.htm (accessed Dec. 16, 2005).

14. Illustrating a definition of fundamentalism that carries a strong negative valuation of it, K. Kienzler quotes the political scientist Thomas Meyer, who says: "Fundamentalism is a wilful movement of seclusion, a protest movement in opposition to the modern process of general openness in thinking, in acting, in life-forms and societies, [promising] absolute security, firm stands, dependable relationships and undisputable orientation by irrational condemnation of all alternatives" (my translation); in K. Kienzler, *Fundamentalismus,* p. 15.

15. See Kienzler, *Fundamentalismus,* pp. 60-63. The two most important texts are the Decrete of the Holy See "Lamentabili" and the Papal Encyclical "Pascendi." For an American source, see *The Encyclopedia of Christianity,* vol. J-O, Erwin Falbusch, ed. (Grand Rapids: Eerdmans, 2003), p. 610.

16. Among the more prominent "victims" of this fundamentalism belong my coun-

Karen Armstrong and Klaus Kienzler have shown that, during this same period, fundamentalist movements began in both Muslim and Jewish circles. The Muslim Brotherhood, for instance, created by the Egyptian Hassan al-Banna in 1928, is just such a movement: its aim was to restore the authority of Islam while it struggled against the colonial and secularizing powers that dominated the Middle East. In a similar fashion, a fundamentalist movement among orthodox Jews formed itself in protest against the religiously indifferent and Zionist motivations for the foundation of an Israeli state. In all these cases, religious fundamentalism appears to be a remedy for people who suffer under injustices, economic inequalities, intellectual contradictions, and moral ambivalences that they find too difficult to bear.

A telling example is the rapid growth of fundamentalist Protestant and charismatic churches in Central and South America. People find refuge in these little *iglesias* and *templos* after they have lost their bearings when forced to migrate from their rural homes to the chaotic "wilderness" of the great city slums. Europeans and North Americans often think of such migratory processes as simply about economic issues. But in reality these dislocations are devastating experiences with deep cultural, social, and religious implications. It is hardly an exaggeration to speak of "end-of-the-world" experiences to which fundamentalist communities address themselves with a simplified message, based on the unfailingly true Bible and a strict code of what to believe and how to behave. We find similar developments and communities everywhere around the world. The impoverishment of large parts of humankind and the chaotic disturbances of their life conditions provide the reasons for the spread of assorted religious fundamentalisms. Conscientious Christians cannot be indifferent to such dislocations and suffering.

Nor is it possible to restrict fundamentalism to religious communities alone. The international debate about the course and future of

_____

trymen and fellow theologians Hans Küng and Eugen Drewermann; in Latin America, Leonardo Boff; and in the United States, Charles Curran and Matthew Fox (who was expelled from the Dominicans).

globalization is marked by a dispute that can also be seen as a struggle between "fundamentalists" and "liberals."[17]

How Does Fundamentalism Work?

It is impossible to provide a comprehensive picture of fundamentalism around the world, nor is it necessary in the context of this book. However, in order for us to understand and overcome the "clash of fundamentalisms" that casts so large a shadow over today's political problems, it may be helpful to identify fundamentalism's most characteristic strategies of belief and action. I suggest these four: *reductionism, authoritarianism, denial accompanied by projection,* and *aggressive violence.*

Reductionism

If it is correct to describe fundamentalisms as pathological reactions to modernity, then reductionism is a way to simplify the complexities that come with the unprecedented increase in data of all kinds. A good example is the complexity surrounding the study and interpretation of the Bible, which has been a major marker of the origins of Protestant and Catholic fundamentalism. Historical-critical research and related investigative methods created the impression among many Christians,

---

17. To quote an example: An international network consisting of the Global Contract Foundation, Global Marshall Plan Foundation, Club of Budapest, Club of Rome, Ökosoziales Forum Europa, Global Society Dialogue have suggested the formation of a Global Marshall Plan. Their proposals for a "Planetary Project" are based on the Millennium Development Goals set forth by the United Nations and aimed at an "eco-social market economy." The scientists involved in these organizations have no doubts that such a project is both urgently needed and financially manageable. However, the promotion is constantly hindered, if not stopped, by international economic and political "hardliners" who insist on the belief that the existing free market system can and will solve the world's problems. This is an "economic fundamentalism" that prevents trial of fresh approaches on a worldwide scale. See Franz-Josef Radermacher, *Global Marshall Plan: Ein Planetary Contract für eine Ökosoziale Marktwirtschaft* (Vienna: Ökosoziales Forum Europa, 2004).

lay and ordained, that Holy Scripture was being cut to pieces, eliminating God's voice while reducing "the Word" to the contributions, transcriptions, and corrections of various authors over a great span of time. What is left when the Bible is reduced to the mechanics of text-making and transmission? Conservative Christians feared that the authority and holiness of the Bible was being destroyed.

To be sure, the interpretive problems of the Bible for human beings of today have become very complex. To the extent that the scientific model reigns, each generation must bring more background to its reading. It has indeed become difficult to find an approach that is simultaneously intellectually honest, spiritually meaningful, and ethically convincing. But the fundamentalist reaction to this dilemma is to drastically reduce the hermeneutical complexities by affirming the inerrancy of Holy Scripture. This is a desperate way to simplify the interpretive tasks: it declares that the truth of the Bible has been "saved" and that those who embrace this view will be free of intellectual doubts and the ensuing spiritual and moral confusion. The fundamentalists frame such a reductionism as "faith" pure and simple; thus faith becomes a matter of obedience, and the believer willingly sacrifices any critical questions in the service of the divine truth.

But is there an alternative? It would be an illusion to pretend that average Christians could manage to live with the full complexities of theological research. All academic theologians and all pastors — and, to an even greater degree, all laypeople — are bound to condense the wealth of available information and relevant interpretations to their levels of comprehension. It has become impossible to take stock of the existing information on even one book of the Bible — Romans, for example — let alone to accommodate the complexities that exist in the theological "market" within one integrated system. If this applies to biblical studies and theology, it is even more true of the interactions of those disciplines with other academic disciplines and the data from the cultural and political realms. A thoughtful person realizes that everyone must select data relevant to his or her religious frame of meaning. All theologians, church leaders, and laypeople must reduce the complex options and viewpoints in order to work with them. If we could not simplify in this way, we would no longer be able to communicate at all. It is natural, therefore, for religious subsystems, such as denominations or regional groups of churches, to communicate on the basis of interpretive networks, accustomed rituals, and frames of meaning that we have agreed to understand in similar ways.

The same is true for people working in the area of politics, or in any other area of human activity for that matter. While it is mandatory for them to elaborate as many relevant data as possible, they also need scenarios (i.e., hermeneutical settings) by which to organize them so that they can derive specific decisions from them.

It is obvious, then, that our modern societies operate, to a certain extent, on reductions and simplifications. What is not as obvious is whether communities, their substructures, and their decision-making leaders know the fact that they are not working on "the truth" but on preliminary scenarios.[18] To the extent that we must know the world in order to live in it, the important requirement is a constant awareness of the need to rework and restructure our scenarios in order to stay in tune with the rapidly changing information. This work of constant reassessment has become a vital ingredient of modern democratic societies. If they fail to remain vigilant in the appropriation of complexities, they will fall prey to individuals, small groups, or media trusts that pretend to do that work for them dispassionately. Once peoples and societies accept the notion that complexity is too difficult to manage or, even worse, a product of evil powers intent on confusing them, they are bound to accept reductionism as the only workable solution. A vigilant and self-critical involvement in the constant reassessment of relevant data is mandatory for functioning societies if they are not to succumb to reductionist "solutions."

Authoritarianism

Once the faithful have accepted reductionism, the need to control possible doubts and hazards rests with those who claim to possess the in-

18. And even the suggestion that this is a fact will be contested by those who believe that the psychological feelings of certainty are sufficient to establish the truth of what is believed.

terpretive power. Again, if we take religious organizations as our reference, there will be spiritual leaders, gurus, or high priests who pretend to "know" the will of God. They establish the hermeneutical system within which the believers must move. Those who traverse the borders of this system of beliefs are "betraying" the cause; they are thus dangerous and perhaps need to be removed. It is essential that such authoritarian spiritual leaders maintain the exclusive right to interpret the will of God, because the radical reduction of data involves an intellectually risky selection of data that could lead to unpleasantly skeptical questions from followers. In the previous chapters I have described the radical reductionism inherent in the construction of apocalyptic end-time scenarios. Their leaders (Hal Lindsey, Pat Robertson, Jerry Falwell, Tim LaHaye, and others) need to claim the exclusive authority to interpret the texts, a claim of a divine calling for which they seem to expect absolute loyalty.

One interesting technique they use to promote this strict — and undemocratic — authoritarianism is to invoke the "father" image and to bolster it with many references to "family values." It is the father's role to assume responsibility for the ways in which the children must be raised. He must lead and the children must obey. This authoritarian structure can easily be enlarged to describe the role of the "heavenly father" over against his earthly fold.

It is obvious that this pattern works not only with religious fundamentalists; it also works in political settings. Once a president has reduced the political complexities — regarding terrorism, for example — to an either-or battle between good and evil, he cannot seriously accept a wide-ranging democratic debate about possible ways to handle this problem. Rather, he will assume the role of the father who says, "Trust me," implying that he knows best. Moreover, he may justify his fatherly posture by referring to a "higher Father" who has guided his decisions to wage war, as President George W. Bush did in an interview with Bob Woodward, which I have also referred to in connection with the winner-loser syndrome in chapter 3.[19]

19. President G. W. Bush took this position when the Iraq War was coming under severe criticism. See Bob Woodward's account based on his interview: "Did Mr. Bush

I would not deny that nations, societies, and religious institutions need "authorities," that is, men and women who are willing and able to accept leadership obligations. It is indispensable to have persons who are courageous enough to accept leadership roles in the face of overwhelming complexities; for they must be the ones who can organize the scenarios for managing complex issues. They must also be the ones to provide the spaces for the constant reappropriation of existing findings in order to work out the adjustments needed in response to changing data. And since it is difficult for people in leadership positions to organize their own critique, democratic societies have correctly based the integrity of their functioning on a system of checks and balances. Authoritarian leaders, especially those who claim divine assistance, are potential hazards to democracies. They can flourish more successfully in cultures that are accustomed to superhero images and thus attuned to granting leaders superhuman qualities and rights.

Denial/Projection

Reductionism and authoritarianism are bound to create considerable stress. While people may be willing to let their leaders do their thinking and deciding for them, they still need to face up to their emotions, their spiritual problems, and their moral dilemmas. This is all the more true in fundamentalist structures. The more influence the faithful attribute to their leaders, the more troublesome it will be for them to deal with their own feelings, passions, and failures. This explains the obsession with sexuality in fundamentalist circles, both Christian and Muslim. For how can one be "born again" and yet remain a "prisoner of the flesh"? The obvious way out is to deny the sin within oneself and to project it onto the other — the stranger or the enemy. Denial

---

ask his father for any advice? I asked the president about this. And President Bush said, 'Well, no,' and then he got defensive about it. Then he said something that really struck me. He said of his father, 'He is the wrong father to appeal to for advice. The wrong father to go to, to appeal to in terms of strength.' And then he said, 'There's a higher Father that I appeal to.'" ("Woodward Shares War Secrets," CBS News [online], April 18, 2004: http://www.cbsnews.com/stories/2004/04/15/60minutes/main612067.shtml [accessed Jan. 18, 2006]).

produces a great deal of unacknowledged anger, which needs to be directed onto the evil powers out there. In earlier segments of this book I have dealt with the power of denial and its divisive impact on one's relationships with others. The demonization of other peoples reveals the profundity of the stress that goes with total obedience to authoritarian leaders. This is most obvious among the apocalyptic end-time scenarios: in their depiction, the "unredeemed" world becomes the playground of the Evil One. And this is the point at which fundamentalisms show their tendency to resort to violence.

Aggressive Violence

The logical consequence of reductionism, authoritarianism, and denial is the urge to go to war against the "forces of darkness" that seem to endanger the precarious security established within fundamentalist systems. And the inherent good-evil dualism of their thought system permits only two options: to convert the "others" or to destroy them, to win them over or to cast them out. This belligerence is clearly demonstrated in end-time novels and film productions such as *Left Behind* — and in their Muslim counterparts. It is also manifest in the Islamic suicide terrorists who are shown on videos with the Quran in one hand and a gun in the other. A similar relentless determination can be found in the "war on terrorism," particularly as seen in President Bush's continued emphasis on "total victory" and his companion argument that "we must confront threats before they fully materialize," which means that we must roam the world in a lethal search for enemies.[20] This search is potentially endless, because the aggressiveness it claims to destroy re-creates itself in every attack.

I do not pretend that these four markers tell the whole story of fundamentalism. But I do think that they help to understand the nature of fundamentalist systems — be they religious, economic, political, or all of the above. With these markers in mind, we can also un-

---

20. Gerry Gilmore, "Bush: U.S. Seeks Total Victory," United States Department of Defense, News Information Service, Aug. 22, 2005: http://www.defenselink.mil/news/Aug2005/20050822_2504.html (accessed Jan. 16, 2006).

derstand the changes in religious and political settings. During the past three decades the world has experienced an unprecedented spread of fundamentalist approaches to the world's needs and dilemmas. Perhaps this is the shadow side of the new wave of globalization that has taken place over the last three decades. And we can also observe it happening in the United States. Although most Americans like to believe in the steady continuity of their country's policies, there have been profound changes that became manifest toward the end of the 1970s. Jimmy Carter is correct when he writes about the "rise of religious fundamentalism" and about "fundamentalism in government" as phenomena that have emerged since he left the White House.[21] Thomas Frank makes a similar observation when he speaks of the "Great Backlash" that swept Ronald Reagan into the White House and enabled the Republican party to consolidate its power base, even in areas that had hitherto been mostly Democrat.[22] On a personal level, I can say this: the "America" I experienced during my year at Yale in 1965 is no longer the "America" I observe today.

At Pains with Modernity: The Protean Self

Fundamentalism is not the only pathological reaction to the acceleration, complexity, and pluralisms of the modern age. The other pathological way to escape its pressures is simply by surrendering oneself to them. This phenomenon has been described in detail by Robert Jay Lifton in his book *The Protean Self*.[23] Proteus is a mythological figure of ancient Greece, the god of many forms and shapes and, through that cosmic role, also the god of the waves. The symbolism suggests that Proteus has no power of his own but derives his might from other powers that propel him. When a heavy storm hits the sea, the waves can be disastrous; when there is but a gentle breeze, the waves subside.

21. Carter, *Our Endangered Values*, pp. 30ff., 94ff.

22. Thomas Frank, *What's the Matter with Kansas? How Conservatives Won the Heart of America* (New York: Metropolitan Books, 2004).

23. Robert Jay Lifton, *The Protean Self: Human Resilience in an Age of Fragmentation* (New York: Basic Books, 1993).

Lifton uses this metaphor when he says: "We are becoming fluid and many-sided. Without quite realizing it, we have been evolving a sense of self appropriate to the restlessness and flux of our time."[24] Lifton goes on to say that the influences that have been contributing to this psychic state can be traced back to the Renaissance period — in other words, to the beginning of the modern age. But Lifton also notes that this "proteanism" has increased in urgency during the second half of the twentieth century. He refers to the "dislocations of rapid historical change, the mass media revolution, and the threat of human extinction. All have undergone an extraordinary acceleration during the last half of the twentieth century, causing a radical breakdown of prior communities and sources of authority."[25]

While the fundamentalist self seeks to save itself in this chaos by holding on to absolute truths and "holy" — and thus unquestionable — sources, the protean self seeks to survive in this general turbulence by becoming fluid and malleable itself. This kind of self renounces the task of reappropriating the inherited systems of meaning, because the challenges and confusions of the modern globalized world appear to have become unmanageable. Hence a protean mentality accepts the modes and trends of our time and follows its impulses and promises without seriously questioning them. There are no strict moral rules to be followed, no personal or social virtues to be adhered to at all costs.

It is difficult to put names and faces to this protean mentality. But we can point to a filmmaker such as Woody Allen, who appears to be playing with the moral and existential problems of women and men. There is nothing that is beyond his ironic, perhaps even cynical, perspective. His movie *Match Point* (2005) is a telling example: it is mere coincidence that the young protagonist gets away with his murder. Coincidence — good luck or bad luck — are the prime movers in people's lives. If that is the case, there is obviously nothing to hold onto.

A second example can be found in the twelve caricatures of the prophet Muhammad that were published in the Danish newspaper *Jyllands Posten* on September 30, 2005. Aside from the fact that this

24. Lifton, *Protean Self*, p. 1.
25. Lifton, *Protean Self*, p. 3.

newspaper is a staunch supporter of the right-wing government led by Fogh Rasmussen and its blatantly xenophobic policies, the publication of these caricatures displays what could well be called "religious illiteracy." Apparently, the journalists involved were not aware of the fact that in Islam the Prophet Muhammad is not to be represented in any picture, let alone be subjected to caricatures of whatever kind. When Muslim fundamentalists in Denmark let the world know of this "blasphemous event," they created an uproar throughout most of the Muslim countries. This led journalists across Europe, notably in France, to publish some or all of the caricatures — both "in solidarity with their Danish colleagues" and in defense of the democratic right of "freedom of expression." This showed very little sensitivity to the religious convictions of Muslim communities. As I write this (in February 2006), many politicians and journalists are revealing a protean naiveté as they appear to be surprised that such a trifling thing should cause such furious and violent reactions in Muslim countries (some of which have been "organized" by extremist groups).

In a peculiar way, the protean perspective mirrors the apocalypticism on the fundamentalist side. For if the prophets of doom are right, why bother? If those who claim that we are all on a *Titanic* that is headed for a deadly collision with the icebergs of nuclear warfare, or ecological winter, or the Battle of Armageddon, or mass death from HIV-AIDS, why care about the state of the world fifty years from now?

This does not mean that protean persons are necessarily bad. They can be very generous, if that is what people do; but they may be quite negligent if other expectations come along. They seem to have no stability of purpose, no endurance in difficult times. The "anything goes" and "let's have fun" attitude prevails. Despite the fact that the entertainment industries and the shopping malls are partial to this kind of mentality, it is a pathological reaction, a form of emotional and intellectual collapse. I introduce the notion of proteanism for two reasons:

(1) Without going into detail, I think we can safely say that proteanism is something we have come to know very well. Most people would certainly agree that the multifaceted and rapidly changing impulses of our daily lives cause all of us to develop a kind of patchwork identity that enables us to accommodate a wide range of modes

and trends. Yet, while we are convinced that openness and plurality are essentially good aspects of our modern world, we struggle with its obvious dangers. Is the protean self resilient enough to make the choices that are constantly necessary? Lifton seems to think so, but he admits that proteanism can and also does turn into a mere reflection of the fragmentation with which it attempts to struggle. He speaks of "dysfunctional proteanism"[26] and of a fragmented self that is "neither centered nor decentered, but *uncentered*."[27]

I am trying to speak with empathy about both proteanism and fundamentalism, because both are realities that are close to us. When I suggest treating both phenomena as pathological reactions to modernity, I do not wish to excuse them and dismiss their danger. Rather, I wish to point out that, in order to deal with them successfully, it is necessary to acknowledge that there is much that is sorely wrong with our modern world. If we wish to overcome both extremes, we must be self-critical as we examine the shortcomings and pitfalls of modernity. We should be concerned about the changes that are necessary for us to overcome both the rigidity of fundamentalism and the fluidity and arbitrariness of proteanism. What can be done to create stable situations in which our children and young people can find their moorings without losing their curiosity? What are the civilizing energies needed to keep our "civilized" world in order? Is there a way somewhere between the captivity of the fundamentalist self and the fragmentation of the protean self?

As a matter of fact, we are not beginning from scratch. Those of us who try to avoid both extremes should affirm that we are in a majority. In the United States, as in Europe and other parts of the world, majorities of the populations are constantly involved in this civilizing work by creating and re-creating the space of confidence and safe grounding that enables them and the coming generations to lead meaningful lives in the midst of — and in spite of — confusion and chaos. In other words, we should not permit the discussion to be dominated by extremist voices.

26. Lifton, *Protean Self*, p. 202.
27. Lifton, *Protean Self*, p. 206.

(2) The second reason why I suggest that we talk about proteanism while dealing with fundamentalism is that there is the danger that fundamentalists denounce everything outside their realm as fluid, chaotic, decadent, and immoral. Simultaneously, there is the danger that proteanists denounce everything that lies beyond their flexibly adaptive impulses as stubborn, inflexible, and fanatical. It appears that the extremes are doing all the talking while the people in between are silent. The public discourse about the visions and values that are to guide a society is being hijacked by the loudspeakers from the fundamentalist and the protean extremes. They introduce a belligerence that drives people further apart, and in so doing they tend to withdraw into opposing subcultures. The result is that both the integrity of societies and the resilience of civilizations are weakened. A disturbing example is the bizarre battle between Muslim groups — notably in the Middle East — and "the West" that was triggered by the Danish caricatures of the prophet Muhammad. The extremists have hijacked the political agendas.

The Fundamentalist Dilemma — Two Examples

Why is fundamentalism so strong in the United States? It cannot be the economic misery that drives many people in Central and South America into fundamentalist circles (though Thomas Frank believes that severe economic changes in parts of the Midwest have contributed to the rise of fundamentalist beliefs).[28] Nor can it be the shaming that causes so many Muslims in Egypt and other Arab countries to take up the fundamentalist positions of the Muslim Brotherhood and similar extremist groups. Yet, if statistics are to be believed, about one-third of the U.S. population follows fundamentalist ideas and practices. Extremely conservative megachurches and their leaders control television and radio stations throughout the country. Why is this? And why do they nurture the impression that they are in a beleaguered state of being, desperately fighting against overpowering enemies within their

28. Frank, *Kansas*, esp. chapter 2.

own country and abroad? One reason, among others, may be that the antagonism in the United States between fundamentalist and protean positions is particularly acute.

Perhaps one can say that the United States is not only the main winner of modernity but also one of its main losers. Although it profits from the latest wave of globalization, it also is confronted with the threatening complexities that this precarious situation entails. Obviously, the advantages and disadvantages of globalized modernity are closely intertwined. America's status as the world's only superpower is on full display in the splendor and affluence of the banks, research centers, and shopping malls, not to mention the bunkers that hide the nuclear missiles; at the same time, its violent underside is glaringly visible in its dilapidated townships and overfilled prisons. The United States is both the leader of the rich nations and, in some ways, a Third-World country. It is vast and anonymous enough to encompass the most bizarre groups and attitudes; everything, from the most noble to the most obscene, seems to be possible — and permissible. Call it hedonism, materialism, or the love of violence, but the contours of freedom and the limits of openness appear to be blurred.

It is not surprising, therefore, that fundamentalists see enemies around every corner and see their "mission" as fighting them wherever they see them. Their evocation of the so-called traditional American family values is an attempt to bring the nation back to its alleged original purity and stability. In other words, the culture war that is currently raging in the United States is led by protagonists of the fundamentalist and proteanist extremes. The pressures on the democratic nature of the American society are considerable. While the fundamentalists follow authoritarian — even theocratic — perspectives, the proteanists could not care less.

In *What's the Matter with Kansas?* Thomas Frank describes in detail how political leaders use the bitterness and resentment of impoverished Americans in places such as Kansas to get them enraged about the snobbery of the "liberals" and the "elites" in the "blue states." They exploit a portrait of America's true and genuine people being surrounded by pornography and decadence. Frank quotes Phil Kline: "So from one coast we hear that the Pledge is unconstitutional, and from the other coast we hear that pornography must be provided to children. . . ."[29] Then a look at the entertainment industries just seems to fuel the fundamentalists' fear and fury. *Brokeback Mountain,* a film featuring two homosexual cowboys, wins the Golden Globe Best Picture award for 2005. The Best Actress award goes to Felicity Huffman, already notorious for her part in *Desperate Housewives,* this time for playing a transgendered person in the movie *Transamerica.* And Philip Seymour Hoffman is chosen Best Actor for his role as the homosexual writer Truman Capote in *Capote.*

These gestures of defiance toward "the normal" can be seen as predictable expressions of the pluralism that is typical in the openness of the U.S. democracy. But for people caught in an either-or mentality, they look like sure indications of a country that is betraying its core values and needs to be set right again — by force, if need be. This is the same either-or dichotomy that I have discussed earlier in this book. It works within the United States and also at the international level: it adds an aggressive note to the exceptionalism that places the United States over against "the rest" of the world. It helps explain the apocalyptic violence of end-time scenarios such as *Left Behind,* and it dominates the superheroic myths of the winner-loser syndrome.

The war on terrorism is the logical political expression of these fundamentalist fixations. The clear-cut options it pretends to offer are the product of a radical reduction of global complexities and injustices to a good-versus-evil dichotomy, which produces a mindset that allows no serious consideration of alternatives. As a result, authoritarian forms of leadership prevail, and massive violence is inevitable. (This violence pertains not only to the battlefield as such but also to prison camps and torture chambers.) Obviously, such fundamentalist violence provokes and deepens violent reactions. This is the vicious cycle of violence and retaliation that gives the "clash of fundamentalisms" its cruel inevitability and forecloses any prospect of peace. The war that President Bush launched against Saddam Hussein's Iraq is a clear product of this fundamentalist dilemma. Despite Bush's triumphant declaration in May 2003 that the invasion's mission had been

29. Frank, *Kansas,* p. 232.

"accomplished," the war goes on and threatens to involve Iraq's neighbors. Even if the United States manages to bring its troops back home, the warring will continue at various grades of intensity. Irreplaceable treasures have been destroyed, and anger and hatred have been aroused that will be difficult to quell in the foreseeable future.

The war against Iraq was named "Operation Iraqi Freedom." It is hardly surprising that many Iraqis experience this kind of freedom as a further act of humiliation. Although most Iraqis will be relieved to see Saddam Hussein in prison, they are not at all happy with the presence of Americans. How is it that there continues to be what Thomas L. Friedman, certainly no friend of the Arab peoples, calls "Saddamism"? He describes this attitude as "a deeply entrenched Arab mindset, born of years of colonialism and humiliation" that insists that upholding Arab dignity and Arab nationalism by defying the West is more important than freedom, democracy, and modernization.[30] In other words, Iraqis are rejecting the promise of the American liberties because that promise does not mean a liberation from years of humiliation.

This leads me to a second example. It starts with a question often raised after 9/11: How is it possible that the young Muslims who hijacked the planes to destroy the Twin Towers and the Pentagon were well-to-do students with excellent prospects? They did not come from impoverished families, nor had they been exposed to desperate and demeaning conditions. In fact, they had all the means to make it even in the Western world. Yet this may have been exactly the reason why they decided to sacrifice their lives in their attempt to kill as many of their "enemies" as possible. My impression is that they found themselves in the acute dilemma of profound uprootedness: on the one hand, they had to appropriate their inherited systems of meaning; on the other, they had to deal with the promises and temptations of the modern world. It is quite possible that they were torn between their fundamentalist selves, that is, the traditional values of their Muslim origins, and their protean selves, that is, the opportunities of the West with its liberal — and libertine — ways of life.

I think it makes sense to assume that this massive dilemma was too

30. Thomas L. Friedman, "The Sand Wall," *New York Times*, April 13, 2003, IV, 13.

difficult for these young men to accommodate. The closer they got to the tempting options of the Western world, the only choice was between giving in to the temptations of the West and "betraying" their inherited culture or fighting those temptations at all costs. Thus they needed to demonize the protean openness of Western democracies, because the wealth of options that those democracies offer appeared to be unmanageable. The only way out seemed to be the fundamentalist withdrawal into the ultimate self-sacrifice, the negation of life in the face of the temptations of a sweet, yet unworthy, existence under the spell of the "American Satan."

In like manner, Muslim fundamentalists need to resolutely reduce the inherent complexity of Islam. They need to ignore the fact that every *Sura* of the Quran begins with the invocation of Allah as the Most Compassionate and the All-Merciful. They dare not contemplate what it means that compassion and mercy are the fundamental motives of Islam. Nor does their extremism provide the space to observe the ethical complexities of their faith. Even in the extreme case of *jihad*, non-combatants — especially women and children — are to be spared. The real Islam, rooted in the Quran, does not know such a thing as "collateral damage." Thus fundamentalist extremism betrays the core of the faith it pretends to save.

How Should We Deal with Fundamentalism?

How, then, are we to overcome fundamentalisms? There are many aspects that come to mind, and my observations will be only a very small contribution to this great task. On the personal level, I would like to emphasize that fundamentalist believers deserve deep respect for their dedication and commitment. It is necessary to acknowledge the pain that many of them feel as they look at the world and its dangers. Even if one is inclined to consider most of these dangers imaginary or exaggerated, it will be important to understand that some are very real. The essential question that the rise of so much fundamentalism provokes is: What are the fundamentals we need in the midst of a disturbingly complex, globalized world? What are the "self-evident truths" that women and men of all cultures and religions at the early stage of the twenty-first century need to appropriate? How can we hold on to — and reconstruct — those values, legal norms, and stable environments that we need in order to create the comprehensive and trustworthy images for a future worth living in the face of the technological acceleration, the increasing intellectual and moral complexities, the growing economic and cultural disparities, and religious antagonisms? These are urgent questions, not any less to people in highly industrialized, economically affluent, and ecologically wasteful societies than they are to so-called Third-World people. Rather than dismissing fundamentalists as irrational and irrelevant, all people of good will should be inspired by their determination to make a determined search for those values and norms that we consider essential to the life of our neighborhoods, our local communities, our democratic societies — that is, our earthly home.

This brings me to the *social* level. The German philosopher Jürgen Habermas is not the only one to raise the question of whether our Western democracies are capable of providing and re-creating the values by which they exist. His response is that the resilience of our democratic systems cannot be taken for granted. Therefore, he argues, the public discourse needs to be invigorated, and toward that end we urgently need to develop a lively civil society.[31] Looking at the United States from a European perspective, this seems all the more necessary because there is no outside power strong enough to challenge the U.S. democratic system. As I have argued earlier, the fundamentalist and protean extremes are narrowing the space in which the public discourse that sustains American democracy can take place. In other words, the only enemies of democracy the people of the United States need to fear come from within.

How do we face the fundamentalist and protean extremes at the *religious* levels? What are the fundamentals on which we can agree together with women and men of other faiths? How are we to re-

31. Jürgen Habermas, *The Future of Human Nature* (Cambridge: Polity Press, 2003); see esp. chapter 3, "Faith and Knowledge" (pp 101-15), which was first published in Habermas's *Glauben und Wissen* (Frankfurt/Main: Suhrkamp Verlag, 2001).

establish the space needed to build sustainable relationships between the world's peoples in response to the powers that drive them apart? What are the images and visions, the symbols and values that enable us to come to terms with the utter vulnerabilities that mark our finite earth? This concern is particularly urgent for those of us who belong to Christian communities. If we are called to be good stewards of creation, how can we uphold this mission in the face of the apocalyptic scenarios of the fundamentalist "credotainment industries," as well as the patchwork religiosity that treats religious beliefs, rituals, and practices like the kinds of goods you might pick up at the shopping mall?

Finally, how can we, as the world's citizens, work toward policies that replace the self-destructive "clash" scenarios with concepts of enduring and sustainable life? I am not sure that people in Germany, or anywhere else in Europe, have found a satisfying answer. Most of them prefer to turn their backs on the messy problems of the world and go about their own business. There is the trend to establish a mentality that sees Europe as a "mighty fortress" that is determined to fend off the people from Africa or Asia who want to climb over the walls. On the other hand, many Europeans know that ours is a small and open-ended continent, close to the conflicts that ravage countries in Eastern Europe and the Middle East. Although many pursue a pragmatic approach that aims at containing the conflict potential and keeping dialogues — and economic relations — open, there are also deep-seated animosities and even xenophobic attitudes that have surfaced in the "war of caricatures" in early 2006.

Obviously, the conflict over the blasphemous content of the caricatures in *Jyllands Posten* must be regarded as a bizarre sideshow to the larger clash in which the United States has the leading part. Even so, it shows us that the European countries cannot pretend to be "neutral" when it comes to facing the questions of how the peoples of this world are going to get along with each other.

While this is a difficult question for Europeans, it may be even more difficult for American citizens. More than their neighbors on this side of the Atlantic, they are accustomed to the triumphalist promises of messianic exceptionality, carried by some to apocalyptic extremes and combined by others with superheroic images of global "überpower."[32] Of course, at the same time, many citizens realize that there is a world out there with enormous problems and challenges. Moreover, there is earth itself showing signs of increasing restlessness, as if its carrying capacities were about to be exhausted. This is the bewildering context within which the two remaining chapters of this book are meant to offer some answers.

32. See Michael Hirsh, *At War with Ourselves* (Oxford/New York: Oxford University Press, 2003), p. 7 and elsewhere. Hirsh rightly traces the term "überpower" to the philosophy of Friedrich Nietzsche without realizing its misuse by the German fascists. Nietzsche spoke of the *Übermensch*, the human being whose power places him/her over and above the rest of humankind. In applying this kind of *Übermenschentum* to American power, Hirsh confirms all the worries of those who have been subjected to it.

CHAPTER 7

The Battle for God in America

—❦—

"**G**od bless America!" The familiarity and ease with which "God" is invoked in the public life of the United States may initially suggest to an outsider that everyone in the nation confidently agrees about the character of this God. But that's just where the problem starts. For Americans, God presents several faces. Some features remind me of Mars, the war-god of ancient Rome. When I look at the Statue of Liberty, Venus, the ancient goddess of love and beauty, comes to mind. Or Marduk, the Babylonian God who created the world out of chaos by redemptive violence, as Walter Wink has suggested. In *Engaging the Powers* he has written that the "myth of redemptive violence undergirds American popular culture, civil religion, nationalism, and foreign policy, and that it lies coiled like an ancient serpent at the root of the system of domination that has characterized human existence since well before Babylon ruled supreme."[1]

It does not suffice, however, to refer to the mythological figures of age-old religions. When Presidents Clinton and George W. Bush speak

1. Walter Wink, *Engaging the Powers: Discernment and Resistance in a World of Domination* (Minneapolis: Fortress Press, 1992), p. 13. See his argument that Marduk is the God whose spirit controls America in *The Powers That Be: Theology for a New Millennium* (New York: Galilee/Doubleday, 1998), esp. pp. 42ff.

about God, they refer to the God of the Bible. But that does not make the question of God's character for Americans any easier for an observer to discern. The "God" in whose authority President Bush went to war against Iraq did not seem to be the same "God" in whose name many Christians opposed this adventure. The United Methodist Church, which counts both President Bush and Vice President Cheney among its members, has been a vocal opponent of that war. In January 2006, ninety-nine bishops and five thousand members signed a statement lamenting "an unjust and immoral invasion and occupation of Iraq." Their concerns have been augmented by those of Catholic bishops in the United States.[2] A friend told me in a private conversation that, according to his estimate, three-quarters of the ordained ministers in the United States opposed Bush-style Christianity, while three-quarters of the people in the pew agreed with it. While such an informal estimate does not match the public polling results, which reveal a rather evenly divided nation, they do point to a divergence between church leaders strongly opposed to the war and parishioners who lukewarmly or fervently endorse the war. And we should add that the Southern Baptists, the largest Protestant denomination in the United States, have offered expressions of support for Bush's "courage and leadership in his valiant opposition to terrorism."[3] Are we to assume, then, that there are at least two kinds of God and two kinds of Christianity in the United States?

About the Use and Abuse of the Bible

We are removed from the time of the composition of the New Testament by almost two thousand years; and many more centuries separate us from the creation of the Hebrew Bible, which Christians call the Old Testament. Whether we admit it or not, our reading of these texts is influenced by this great distance. And it is not this historical

2. "Methodist group calls Iraq war 'unjust, immoral,'" CNN Online, Jan. 26, 2006: http://edition.cnn.com/2006/US/01/25/churches.iraq.reut.

3. "Methodist group calls Iraq war 'unjust, immoral.'"

distance alone that matters; there are many layers of interpretation that intervene between us and ancient Scripture. These interpretive layers have influenced us in ways we often find hard to understand and harder still to admit, even when we do recognize them. Those who take the trouble to study Hebrew, Greek, and Latin will quickly realize that even the translations of the original texts contain interpretations and thus shifts of meaning. How are we to know whether our word "peace" corresponds to what the people of ancient Israel meant when they spoke of *shalom?* The same applies to other key concepts, such as justice, covenant, love, and honor. The French proverb *traduir c'est trair* ("to translate is to betray") is particularly true when it comes to the Hebrew word *ruah,* which has been translated into "spirit" (in French *ésprit,* in Spanish *espíritu*). The English frame of meaning that goes with the concept of "spirit" has nothing in common with the Hebrew frame of meaning for *ruah.* In the Hebrew language, *ruah* is a feminine reality, while "spirit" is masculine. *Ruah* connotes "storm," "breath," and "life," and hence it points to the energy of life, the power residing in all things. On the other hand, our understanding of "spirit" has been shaped by the dualistically flavored Greek word *pneuma,* which suggests something that can be separated from our bodies, senses, and emotions.

In Christianity's history various traditions of interpretation and their related hermeneutical schools have evolved. Here I will mention only the two that seem most frequently used in the American and European churches of today: the existential and the political. The existential hermeneutic relates the biblical texts mainly to the existential problems of human beings, such as mortality, love, the meaning of life, despair, anxieties, and so forth. The political hermeneutic (of which there are various traditions) relates the biblical stories — the Exodus of the Israelites from Egypt, for example — to the stories of a nation. To give one example: the "covenant" motif that guides the Exodus story has been used to describe the special relationship of a nation to God. As Richard T. Hughes has explained so clearly in *Myths America Lives By,* the "covenant" concept for "the Chosen Nation" reflected an understanding of God's relationship with England during the English Reformation.[4] Thus this hermeneutical frame existed before the Pilgrim fathers took it with them to the New Land and reappropriated it there in the light of their new experiences. They saw themselves within a typological frame that made the ancient story of Israel analogous to their own experiences in conquering the wilderness. They were "the Chosen People in the Promised Land."[5]

It is the assumption in the fundamentalist circles of Judaism, Islam, and Christianity that difficult hermeneutical problems can be overcome by proclaiming the inerrancy of the holy texts. If those texts are divinely inspired, their meaning will be self-evident and thus beyond the whims and wishes of human interpretation. In this way, those who regard themselves as "true believers" of the Bible, the Quran, or the Torah claim to have found a position according to which they can dismiss the hermeneutical questions as sure signs of faithlessness, unnecessary doubt, and sophisticated evasiveness.

As I have pointed out above, hermeneutical problems can lead — and in the past have led — to a protean arbitrariness that takes the Bible as an assortment of more or less relevant ancient texts with no direct importance for life today. On the other hand, the biblically literalist notion that the truth of the Bible is self-evident and needs only to be directly applied in today's life is an illusion. It goes without saying that even those who interpret the Bible "literally" and believe in its inerrancy do not take all the parts of the Bible as equally important or normative. If they did, they would have to do a lot of stoning to death. If they took Leviticus 20 literally, for example, they would have to impose the death penalty for sins such as cursing one's parent or having sexual relations with a neighbor's wife, or sexual relations with a person of the same sex, or sodomy. If they took other Old Testament passages literally and as normative for faith and practice, they would be allowed to practice polygamy but would have to send their wives outside the city every time they had a menstrual period. One need only read Deuteronomy 20–25 to see the host of strange, even bizarre, bibli-

---

4. Hughes, *Myths America Lives By* (Urbana/Chicago: University of Illinois Press, 2003), pp. 20-28.

5. Hughes, *Myths*, pp. 28-33.

cal injunctions that even the most literalist of believers today do not embrace or practice.

In other words, biblical literalists select texts and leave out others according to their preferences and missionary goals. One particularly outrageous example of this selectivity came to my attention in the first days of 2006. When Israel's Prime Minister Ariel Sharon suffered a series of strokes, the Reverend Pat Robertson picked out a few words from the prophet Joel (4:2) and inferred that God's wrath had struck down a man "who had divided the land of God" by removing Jewish settlements from the Gaza strip.[6] The inerrancy hypothesis enables fundamentalists such as Robertson to proudly dismiss the Bible's hermeneutical complexities, with the consequence, of course, that they claim a certain level of inerrancy for themselves.

Christian fundamentalists also overlook the fact that the four Gospels in the New Testament reveal a considerable amount of divergence regarding the life, witness, and death of Jesus Christ. This is an excellent example of the freedom and sovereignty with which leaders of the early church accepted the hermeneutical challenges implied by the Christian faith when they determined what was to be the content of the New Testament. Against the reductionist position of Marcion, who wanted to admit only one Gospel, Luke, and a sharply reduced number of the Pauline Epistles, the early church opted for a diverse approach — including even the very controversial Revelation of St. John as the last canonical book.[7]

There is no need to go into the diverting details of these early arguments about what belongs in the Bible. It is more to the point to show that a similar process has taken place within Islam. The relative open-

6. Alan Cooperman, "Iranian leader, evangelist call prime minister's illness deserved," *Washington Post*, Jan. 6, 2006, p. A12.

7. Marcion was an influential figure in the second century. His sharp reductionism regarding the content and scope of the New Testament is linked to his Gnostic dualism, which led him to separate the Hebrew God of judgment from Christ as the new God of mercy. See H. Kraft, "Marcion," *Religion in Geschichte und Gegenwart*), 3rd ed., vol. IV (Tübingen: Mohr, 1957-1965), pp. 740-42; see also L. Vischer, "Kanon, Kirchengeschichtlich," *RGG*, 3rd ed., vol. III, pp. 1119-23. For an American source, see Bart D. Ehrman, *The New Testament: A Historical Introduction to Early Christian Writings* (New York: Oxford University Press, 1997), pp. 7-11.

ness of the early decades in which the Quran took its final shape while further interpretive materials emerged has been steadily replaced by fundamentalist restrictions on the potential meanings of Islam's holy book. It is clear that this reductionism is allied with authoritarian structures that are designed to guarantee "orthodoxy" and suppress divergent views, sometimes using very violent means.[8] The fundamentalist refusal to recognize and openly engage in the inevitable hermeneutical processes is an indication of their failure to respond creatively to the complexities of our heritage as well as our present situation. In the case of the fundamentalists in the United States, it is a kind of failure that brings the ongoing work on the "American experiment" to a standstill.

What does this have to do with "God-talk" in the United States? As we have seen earlier, the Pilgrims perceived the biblical God as the one who had established a covenant with them. This gave them special obligations and rights, which they often understood as the entitlement to acquire the land of the "heathen" Indians and to expel them from it. Somewhat later in American history, the Deists among the Founding Fathers, such as Washington and Jefferson, formulated policies of the new United States that were a creative appropriation of earlier views of "America's mission." They used enlightenment categories to interpret the biblical images of God by speaking of the "highest Being," of "Providence," and the "Lord of History." The aggressive and expansionist paradigm of "manifest destiny" that shaped American conquest in the nineteenth century contributed toward a view that came close to identifying God with the American cause.

The Darbyist interpretation of the Bible put another layer on it. It favored the apocalyptic texts and constructed from them the end-time

8. A telling example is the "death sentence" that was set in motion by Ayatollah Khomeini against the Indian-born Muslim writer Salman Rushdie after his *The Satanic Verses* had been published. Interestingly, the imams of the English city of Bradford were the first to sound the alarm, not least because they feared that their Muslim communities were threatened by absorption into the "proteanism" of secularized British society. For details, see Klaus Kienzler, *Der Religiöse Fundamentalismus: Christentum, Judentum, Islam* (München: Beck, 2001), pp. 80ff.; see also Jewett and Lawrence, *Captain America and the Crusade Against Evil*, pp. 304ff.

scenarios that turned God into a wrathful Supreme Being, with Christ as his superheroic avenger and brave Americans as his earthly combatants. As we have seen from the works of Jewett and Lawrence, the mythological figure of the superhero has found its way into this image of God. This is the violent face that "America's God" presents to the world. Thoroughly masculine, he is a God of stern fatherly power, a God of merciless revenge who destroys the "empires of evil" and calls his chosen people to enter into this global cleansing with joyful fury, a God of war who claims bloody sacrifices.

As negative and unappealing as this image of God may be, it can be traced back to biblical sources. Jewett and Lawrence indicate that it is associated with the "zealous nationalism" that can be found in various parts of the biblical canon.[9] According to these scholars, an example of prototypical relevance can be detected in Numbers 25, which tells the story of a certain Phinehas, who killed an Israelite and his Midianite wife by thrusting them through with his javelin. The justification offered in the text is that they had violated Israel's purity and brought about a plague as God's punishment. The generalizing theory drawn from this story, Jewett and Lawrence argue,

> has had a long and deadly impact: it assumed that reverses suffered by the chosen people, whether sickness, famine, or defeat, were due to divine wrath against internal enemies. The traitor within the camp became the source of evil. Therefore, to rid the chosen people of such internal sources of corruption was to save the nation. The zealot became the redeemer, cleansing the nation by violence so that its triumphant destiny could be restored.[10]

Jewett and Lawrence contrast this "zealous nationalism" with the stance of "prophetic realism" as represented, among others, by the prophet Isaiah.[11] "Prophetic realists experience creative freedom and

9. Jewett and Lawrence, *Captain America,* esp. pp. 45ff., 61ff., 155ff., 168ff.
10. Jewett and Lawrence, *Captain America,* p. 169.
11. Jewett and Lawrence, *Captain America,* pp. 313ff.

are stimulated by a vision of transcendent justice. Their aim is more modest than that of the zealots: it is not to eliminate the crisis but to advance gradually through it toward the goal, always realizing that it may never be fully reached."[12]

The God of Lincoln and the God of Bush

Are the images of divine wrath and divine justice mutually exclusive? Jewett and Lawrence point to President Abraham Lincoln as their chief witness in arguing that these contrasting concepts can and in fact must be held together. In his second inaugural address, Lincoln pointed to the fact that both parties engaged in the devastating Civil War were reading the same Bible and praying to the same God — for opposite blessings and opposite results, obviously. Lincoln drew the conclusion that neither side was in a position to claim divine protection. In reality, the war, with the suffering it had brought, was *in itself* God's judgment on both parties:

> Yet, if God wills that it [the war] continue, until all the wealth piled by the bondsman's two hundred and fifty years of unrequited toil shall be sunk, and that every drop of blood drawn with the lash, shall be paid by another drawn with the sword, as was said three thousand years ago, so still it must be said, "the judgments of the Lord are true and righteous altogether."[13]

So Lincoln was not afraid to admit the reality of guilt in the life of his nation. From his reading of the prophetic pronouncements in the Bible, he knew that God makes no distinction between a slave and his master, that every drop of blood is equally important, that every human being shares the same God-given dignity. For him, God was the ultimate Being, the one to whom the winners as well as the losers of all

12. Jewett and Lawrence, *Captain America*, p. 314.

13. "The Second Inaugural Address of Abraham Lincoln, 4 March 1865," The Avalon Project of Yale University Law School: http://www.yale.edu/lawweb/avalon/presiden/inaug/lincoln2.htm.

earthly battles are held responsible. For that reason he insisted that, once the war had ended, the entire nation was to engage in what might well be called reconciliation politics:

> With malice toward none; with charity for all; with firmness in the right, as God gives us to see the right, let us strive to finish the work we are in; to bind up the nation's wounds; to care for him who shall have borne the battle, and for his widow, and his orphan — to do all which may achieve and cherish a just, and a lasting peace, among ourselves, and with all nations.

Here was an American politician whose awe-inspiring understanding of God transcends the winner-loser divide. Lincoln knew that the only response inherent to accepting the war as God's judgment on all parts of a nation was a policy of mercy and healing. He was realistic enough to understand that a just and lasting peace could not be achieved by (the illusion of) destroying evil but by caring for those who had suffered most.

The God of President Bush, however, does not show this mercy. The president offered no word to indicate that the attacks of 9/11 might also include an element of divine judgment on the policies of the United States. Had not the CIA supported men such as Osama bin Laden while they fought against the Soviet Union? Had not the United States backed Saddam Hussein financially and militarily as he launched his disastrous war against Iran — because then it fit into U.S. plans to put pressure on Ayatollah Khomeini? Not a word of shame or sense of responsibility was to be found in all the pronouncements of American and European leaders after the attacks on the Twin Towers and the Pentagon. Instead, what dominated the speeches were self-righteous indignation and angry cries for retaliation.

For me, as a theologian, one of President Bush's statements is particularly revealing. One year after 9/11, on September 11, 2002, he said in a speech at Ellis Island:

> Ours is the cause of human dignity, freedom guided by conscience and guarded by peace. This ideal of America is the hope

of all mankind. That hope still lights our way. And the light shines in the darkness. And the darkness will not overcome it. God bless America![14]

It is not the blatant messianism that jumps out as much as the direct quote from the Gospel of John (1:5). There one reads that he (i.e., Jesus) is the light that shines in the darkness and that the darkness will not overcome it. What is said of Jesus as "the light of all people" Bush directly attributes to the "ideal" of America. This identification is revealing: he transfers the salvation through Jesus Christ, toward which Christians set their hope, to America itself. "This ideal of America" is, in Bush's thinking, "the hope of all mankind." In other words, the salvation of all humankind depends on America.

This identification of "America's ideal" with Jesus Christ borders on idolatry. While it was clear for Lincoln that the United States was strictly "under" God, Bush sees his "America" functioning at the same level with Christ. America's "ideal" takes on the role of Christ and is as victorious as the Risen One.[15] I find this blending of christological and national images frightening — both as a theologian and as a German. It may no doubt flatter many U.S. citizens, especially the fundamentalists among them, for whom religious and patriotic sentiments appear to be one. But the blasphemous elements are there. "America" becomes a God-like reality with the attributes

14. George W. Bush, "President's Remarks to the Nation, Ellis Island, NY, September 11, 2002" (White House release: http://www.whitehouse.gov/news/releases/2002/09/20020911-3.html [accessed Jan. 22, 2006]).

15. Samuel Huntington says: "The flag, as many scholars have pointed out, became essentially a religious symbol, *the equivalent of the cross for Christians*" [italics added] (*Who Are We? America's Great Debate* [London: Simon & Schuster, 2004], p. 129). Further, he says: "Two words . . . do not appear in civil religion statements and ceremonies. They are 'Jesus Christ.' While the American Creed is Protestantism without God, *the American civil religion is Christianity without Christ*" (p. 107 [italics added]). In light of this observation, it seems very odd to me that Huntington says: "America is thus by a large margin the most religious Protestant country. The legacy of its Reformation origins was alive and well at the end of the twentieth century" (p. 92). If anything, the Reformation was about the rediscovery of the centrality of Christ; hence, it seems to me, Huntington's "American civil religion" betrays the legacy of the Reformation.

of divine salvation, redemptive powers, and, if need be, relentless punishment.[16]

America's Battle for God

I realize that my argument here will be hard to swallow for many Americans, especially since it comes from an outsider. But what I have been saying reflects a viewpoint and a struggle that has already begun within the United States. Earlier in this book I referred to Jim Wallis's book *God's Politics,* an impressive example of this battle. He takes issue with the fundamentalist merger of the Christian faith with nationalist, capitalist, and selectively moral concerns: "How did the faith of Jesus come to be known as pro-rich, pro-war, and only pro-American?"[17] Wallis was a very lonely voice in recognizing the idolatry of President Bush's speech at Ellis Island. And his entire book can be read as an attempt to bring the prophetic realism of the Bible to bear on the zealous fundamentalist syncretism by which those practicing American civil religion have turned America into a quasi-divine entity. What strikes me, however, is the fact that Wallis does not appear to have problems with American messianism, though it is the underlying mythological construct that facilitates the merger of faith with patriotism, capitalism, and selective moralism. Nor do I find in Wallis's book the much-needed challenge to the "doom-boomers" of the *Left Behind* persuasion, for it is their apocalyptic zealotry that makes the merger of religion and nationalism especially dangerous.

Another example of a too-limited critique can be found in "God's Earth is Sacred: Open Letter to Christians in the United States," which was written in the early months of 2005 by a group of Orthodox, Catholic, and Protestant theologians convened by the National Coun-

16. In chapter 1, I referred to the importance of the American flag. The political efforts to enact a constitutional amendment banning "flag desecration" are an example of the attempts to turn the flag into a sacred symbol. Since it is the most important symbol of the United States, it links the sacredness of God to that of a sacred nation. For details, see Jewett and Lawrence, *Captain America,* pp. 297ff.

17. Wallis, *God's Politics,* p. 3.

cil of Churches in the United States. The leadership of the Standing Conference of Canonical Orthodox Bishops in the Americas (SCOBA) released the "Open Letter" on July 8, 2005, and its main focus is the environmental damage caused by the affluent lifestyles in the United States (as well as in Europe, one should add); it also clearly addresses the "false gospel" that justifies the abuse of the earth and its riches:

> We have become un-creators. Earth is in jeopardy at our hands. This means that ours is a theological crisis as well. We have listened to a false gospel that we continue to live out in our daily habits. . . . This false gospel still finds its proud preachers and continues to capture its adherents among emboldened political leaders and policy makers.[18]

The term "false gospel" is revealing: for theologians it sounds an alarm, because it says nothing less than that the true gospel is being repudiated or replaced. And wherever the true gospel is being abused and perverted, the Christian faith itself is at stake and needs to be defended. Thus the "Open Letter" addresses itself to a heretical situation and constitutes what theologians call the *status confessionis,* that is, the moment in history when the faith in the true gospel requires active resistance (to the point of martyrdom) against the preachers of the false gospel and those political leaders who are "emboldened" by it.

A comparable note is struck in a confessional statement that was written by the team of Richard Hays (Duke Divinity School), George Hunsinger (Princeton Theological Seminary), Richard V. Pierard (Gordon College), Glen Stassen (Fuller Theological Seminary), and Jim Wallis (*Sojourners* magazine).[19] They observe that "a 'theology of war' is emanating from the highest circles of American government," that "the language of 'righteous empire' is employed with growing fre-

18. "SCOBA Hierarchs Endorse Statement on the Environment, "God's Earth is Sacred: An Open Letter to Christians in the United States," SCOBA News (online): http://www.scoba.us/news/newsdetail.asp?id=137 (accessed July 28, 2005).

19. "Confessing Christ in a World of Violence," *Hospitality* 24, no. 1 (Jan. 2005): 3, 10. The text and the list of signers is also posted at the *Sojourners* website: http://www.sojo.net/index.cfm?action=action.election&item=confession_signers.

quency," and that "the roles of God, church, and nation are confused by talk of an American 'mission' and 'divine appointment' to 'rid the world of evil.'"[20] Therefore, the authors claim, "a new confession of Christ" is needed. In five affirmations they express fundamental aspects of Christ's teaching. Each affirmation is followed by the classical formula, "We reject the false teaching . . . ," which then singles out the heretical distortions of the faith.[21]

This is the spiritual battle that concerns a growing number of Christians in the United States.[22] Referring to it, the German theologian Hans Eckehard Bahr, whose thinking has been deeply influenced by early contacts with Martin Luther King, Jr., talks about two kinds of "religion" in the United States. He distinguishes between "Religion I," that is, the global power-religion of the Bush administration, backed up by the fundamentalist megachurches, and "Religion II," the "human-rights-religion" of many Christian churches.[23] Religion I is characterized by a "friend-foe fanaticism," a "false messianic world order," and an apocalyptic "final solution" approach to the powers of evil. Religion II, the religion of the "other America," is the "flowering of a public democratic discourse" in the civil rights movement, the "table of brotherhood," and the voice of "pragmatic pacifism" that is critical of the powers that be but speaks for the voiceless.

Are these nothing more than the typical quarrels of theologians? I do not believe so. This battle for God is simultaneously a battle for the political, social, and cultural images that govern the hopes and fears of

20. "Confessing," p. 3.

21. Incidentally, the structure of this "confession" follows that of the famous "Barmen Declaration" of the Confessing Church of 1934, which became the basic document for Protestant Christians and congregations in their resistance against Hitler's régime.

22. A remarkable example of this anguish can be seen in the statement that representatives of U.S. churches addressed to their fellow Christians from around the world gathered at the 9th Assembly of the World Council of Churches in Porto Alegre in February 2006. It contains elements of a declaration of guilt and an apology. See *A Letter from the US Conference for the World Council of Churches to the 9th Assembly of the World Council of Churches, Porto Alegre, February 18, 2006:* www.wcc-usa.org/newscontainer/article/1099/a-letter-from-the-US-conf. (accessed March 8, 2006).

23. Hans Eckehard Bahr, *Erbarmen mit Amerika. Deutsche Alternativen* (Berlin: Aufbau-Verlag, 2003).

the citizens of the United States. And these images inform the values that U.S. citizens adhere to and the issues to which they give — or do not give — their attention. As long as the violent God of America's "überpower" appears to be in total control, those who reject him as a false idol will have a very hard time of it indeed.

Choose Life, Not Death: Searching for Global Fundamentals

Because of the idol's power, it is important to work on alternatives. The "confession" that Hays, Hunsinger, Stassen, Wallis, and others have introduced into the debate is a very significant step. Its focus on Jesus Christ and his universal message leads to five significant affirmations about national life:

(1) "Our allegiance to Christ takes priority over national identity."[24] This statement leads to a rejection of any compromise of Christianity with empire.

(2) "Christ commits Christians to a strong presumption against war." Consequently, "international cooperation" is more important than "unilateral policies." With this affirmation they reject "a war on terrorism (that) takes precedence over ethical and legal norms."

(3) "Christ commands us to see not only the splinter in our adversary's eye, but also the beam in our own." This leads to the affirmation that good and evil lie in every human heart. Obviously, this insight rejects as "false teaching" any assumption that America as a "Christian nation" does not need repentance.

(4) "Christ shows us that enemy-love is the heart of the gospel." Consequently, they reject the demonization of perceived enemies as well as any kind of mistreatment.

(5) "Christ teaches us that humility is the virtue befitting forgiven sinners." This leads them to reject the "Manichaean heresy" that "divides the world into forces of absolute good and absolute evil."

24. This and the following quotes are from the text "Confessing Christ in a World of Violence."

In conclusion this confession makes clear that "no nation-state may usurp the place of God."

This is a bold statement indeed. In identifying central aspects of the gospel of Christ, it speaks out against some key elements of America's "war-god-religion." I am certain that many Christians all over the United States will be comforted and encouraged by the spiritual guidance offered in this confession. Yet, from my outsider's perspective, it is too situational and, if I may say so, too narrow. Its context is President Bush's "false teaching" that sees the "war on terrorism" as a divinely ordained mission. There can be no doubt that this nationalistic zealotry must provoke the uncompromising resistance of Christians in the United States. But there is a broader context, and it requires a broader response. As I tried to show in the preceding chapter, the fundamentalism of the extremely conservative right in the United States (whose influence on the Bush administration is evident) is but one expression of the global reality of fundamentalist beliefs. I have also indicated that this pandemic growth reveals deep fault lines that endanger our global situation. Therefore, a broad stand against these varied fundamentalist tendencies is necessary in order to address the most alarming distortions of our epoch:

(1) The factual end-time threat of all-out self-destruction due to the availability of nuclear warheads to a variety of nations and the global spread of nuclear power plants;

(2) the climate change due to global warming that is already underway, along with its full disastrous impact, which will affect generations of our children and grandchildren;

(3) the increasing inequities within the global economic order and, by implication, the increased danger of relentless warfare over access to, and use of, vital resources such as crude oil, natural gas, and water;

(4) the growing confrontations between state-controlled military power and smallscale "mafiosa-type" terrorist activity, with an ensuing loss of legal and related standards of civilization.

Each of these four global threats, taken separately, is depressing enough to quench the hope of human beings in a future worth living.

Taken together, they are capable of eroding the spiritual and intellectual energies needed to continue working for a meaningful and sustainable world. For me, this is the broad context within which the search for "global fundamentals" needs to be situated. To be sure, this search requires the wisdom and courage of men and women of all religions, not only of the Christian faith. If there ever was a need for a truly ecumenical movement to witness to the essential values in which people around the earth can put their confidence and on which they can build their hopes, it is now. To advance this search, I would like to submit the following reflections:

1. The first commandment of the Decalogue is a perfect start because Christians and Muslims have inherited it from their Jewish mother-religion. It prohibits humans from making any image in the likeness of God. What we call "God" is above all the names, images, and concepts we can think of. Even when Muslims and Christians believe that this God has revealed "Godself" in the prophet Muhammad or in Jesus as the Christ, they still affirm God's transcendence. One way to express this utter distance is the notion of holiness: God, the transcendent mystery/reality, is the holy one. No human being can ever be called holy in this ultimate sense, and there most certainly can never be such things as "holy wars." The namelessness of God leads to a marked reticence with regard to our own understanding of God. At the same time, it leads to a profound respect for the faith of people of other religions. When it comes to facing the mysteries of God — the "fundamental" source of both humility and respect — each of us stands with empty hands.

2. Christians believe that everything owes its being to this Supreme Being. Therefore, our ancient creed calls God the "creator of heaven and earth." This means that creation is a reality never to be fully grasped by human understanding. Whatever methods and scenarios we can design to bring order to the overwhelming multitude of phenomena, ranging from the farthest galaxies to the most minute elements within an atom, they remain approximations and need to be understood as such. This is not an obscurantism that defies scientific work; on the contrary, the more profound scientific work gets, the deeper the recognition that life is surrounded and sustained by "net-

works of wonder." Therefore, Christians feel at home in this universe, sustained by a love that passes all understanding.

This is constant reason for awe and admiration, humility and gratitude. The deep receptivity for the networks of wonder creates what I would call a mystic awareness of the fundamental connectedness of all things created. This love of life must be opposed to any kind of fascination with death. It abhors each single suicide bombing just as it abhors the annihilating fantasies of end-time apocalypticists.

3. Christians believe that creation is full of God's blessing and yet torn apart by evil. Why this should be so is impossible to understand and difficult to endure. This is what causes "shock and awe,"[25] not least because evil and guilt are found in every human being. The Bible deals with this terrible fact in its first pages when it tells the mythical story of Cain slaying his brother. The gift of freedom, of which human beings are rightfully proud, carries within it the seed of stinging envy and greed. The awareness of many choices implies the threat of a multitude of dependencies. There is no clear way of separating the will to do good from the seeming inexorability of doing evil.

This, too, is a fundamental, and it is why Christians are moral realists. They do not deny the evil within themselves; and they attempt to avoid projecting it onto others. As much as they try to refrain from evil acts, they must admit their need for redemption. Therefore, Christians turn to Jesus Christ, not only because in him they find the example of a fellow human being free from greed and envy, but much more because he retained his unconditional love even in the face of death. Accepting this love is the source of redemption. Hence Christians seek to be close to this Christ; they re-member him in their prayers and rituals (especially the Eucharist). In Christ a fundamental truth becomes apparent: that the liberation from the burden of guilt and the pressures of humiliation is an option built into creation, and thus it is an opportunity for all human beings, no matter how complex their conflicts may be.

---

25. To use the ominous slogan that surfaced in how the U.S. military expressed hopes for their mission in Iraq in 2003 — to smother all resistance with overwhelming technology and precision explosives.

4. This explains why Christians place history under the category of *metanoia* (the Greek literally suggests a shift of the mind, a change and a conversion). Each captivity can be ended; no dead end is too narrow to make a full turn impossible. There is no guilt too big to be forgiven. Nor is there a conflict too inextricable to make a solution unthinkable. The creative energies of the Creator and the reconciling powers of Jesus, the Messiah, unfold themselves in the presence of what Christians call the Holy Spirit and what the Bible calls the *ruah,* the life-giving, life-sustaining "power in between all things."

The energies of the *ruah* are messianic because they manifest the energy of the crucified Messiah. Therefore, the energies of the *ruah* do not orient themselves to the claims of omnipotence that are so typical of superheroes past and present; rather, they orient themselves to the experiences of the powerless, which are so typical of the vast majority of the world's peoples. The power of the *ruah* of God sustains the *memoria passionis,* the remembrance of suffering, a central term in the work of the German theologian Johann Baptist Metz.[26] Metz places suffering at the center, not because he wants to glorify it, but because suffering is an experience fundamental to all human existence. I agree with him on this point: his term "suffering" is close to what I have earlier described as "vulnerability," a fundamental reality in the lives of all peoples (and a concept I seek to free from its negative connotations). Surely, vulnerability is often exploited and abused by the powerful; yet it is the place where all creative beginnings originate.

Vulnerability is a universal reality. Whenever it is accepted with respect, it unites human beings and enables them to work on systems of sustenance and support, including securities of the legal and social kind. When people realize that their connectedness is grounded in their shared vulnerability, they can overcome the divisions that separate genders, cultures, and races. This relates closely to my concept of deep remembering: it is the capacity to remember both the hurtful as well as the joyful moments in our lives. It sharpens our awareness of the origins of our conflicts and opens our minds to the opportunities of change and conversion.

26. Johann Baptist Metz, *Zum Begriff der Politischen Theologie, 1967-1997* (Mainz: Grünewald, 1997).

5. Lastly, it is a fundamental experience of Christians that they form a worldwide community, for it is the unifying energy of the Messiah that holds them together across all the divides that otherwise place people in separate camps. It is sadly true that Christianity has gone through periods of bitter estrangements and religious wars; but it is also fair to say that the twentieth century has been marked by fresh attempts to discover the connectedness of the various churches and to find appropriate expressions for this growing unity. This remains the great achievement of the modern ecumenical movement.

However incomplete these efforts are, they manifest the fundamental insight that no Christian possesses the truth of the gospel for himself or herself. The truth of the gospel manifests itself only in communion with others. For the truth of the gospel is love. As everyone who has ever been in love knows, that cannot be owned but must be shared. Thus the New Testament speaks of Christians as belonging to the *family* of God: Christian congregations are conceived of as households in which all members support each other. From the beginnings of the apostolic church it was understood that those Christian communities would form networks of mutual help. This implied that they were to settle their disputes in synods and councils, all the way up to the global level (the records of the first Christian council can be found in Acts 15). Such a network of exchange and sustenance must be as "thick" as possible so that it enables all who belong to it to share in the gifts of the others and to contribute to their needs. Even the Pope in Rome realizes that he depends on a critical exchange with bishops around the world and, through them, with the faithful in the local communities. Therefore, it is impossible for individuals, be they preachers, televangelists, or presidents, to pretend to know the will of God without consulting with other members of the Christian communities.

Needless to say, these five "fundamentals" are simply my suggestions toward a search that needs to go on within many organizations that have a capacity to represent broad constituencies of human need and hope. It would also be important for people of other religions to involve themselves in this search, even if their approaches would seem incompatible at first sight. In all cases, the really important thing is not how human beings formulate their fundamentals but the intensity with which they live them. "Fundamentals" are worthless unless they are lived out in sustaining and comforting communities.[27] The task of those communities is to intensify the networks of meaning that enable the coming generations to find their place in society without losing themselves in protean arbitrariness or authoritarian exclusiveness. In practical terms, to cultivate their nurturing and parenting capacities, men and women require sustaining neighborhoods and good educational and training institutions; fair working conditions and honest pay; stable legal systems and reliable public services; clean water, healthy food, and a sustainable environment. In fact, what I have listed here has been elaborated much more carefully by several declarations of individual and social human rights, such as the United Nations' "Declaration of Human Rights" of 1948.

In many ways my interest in a list of fundamentals that could speak to the disparate conditions of our globalized situation is related to the work of international religious organizations such as the Parliament of the World's Religions. To refer to the most important example of its challenge, the 1993 Parliament in Chicago formulated four "irrevocable directives" and commitments:

(1) a culture of nonviolence and respect for life;
(2) a culture of solidarity and a just economic order;
(3) a culture of tolerance and a life of truthfulness;
(4) a culture of equal rights and partnership between men and women.[28]

The main preparatory draft was written by the theologian Hans Küng.[29] He has often summed up his program in three straightforward

27. For more details, see Geiko Müller-Fahrenholz, *God's Spirit Transforming a World in Crisis* (New York: Continuum, 1995), esp. Part III, pp. 108-70.

28. *Declaration Toward a Global Ethic,* Parliament of the World's Religions, Chicago, Sept. 4, 1993 (posted by the Council for the Parliament of the World's Religions: http://www.cpwr.org/resource/ethic.pdf [accessed Jan. 22, 2006]).

29. See esp. Küng, *Global Responsibility: In Search of a New World Ethic* (New York: Crossroad, 1991).

sentences: "No survival without a world ethic. No world peace without peace between the religions. No peace between the religions without dialogue between the religions."[30] This sounds like a simple program, but in reality it is a daring project to which Küng has devoted his monumental energies for more than twenty years.

It is easy to dismiss the work of Küng and that of the Parliament of the World's Religions as diversions into political romanticism. As a matter of fact, what happened a little more than a decade ago in Chicago seems impossible today. The changes in the global political and economic climate have been profoundly polarizing. The confrontational character that pollutes so many international problems has sharply increased since the terrorist attacks of September 11, 2001, in New York and Washington. This applies especially to the relationships within and between predominantly Christian and Muslim societies. Can this trend be stopped and possibly reversed? The story of the Jesuit priest Paolo Dall'Oglio points in that direction and is thus a source of hope.

In 1977, Paolo Dall'Oglio was sent to Lebanon by his general superior, the famous Pedro Arrupe, to study Arabic and Muslim culture. Together with an international group of monks and nuns, Paolo revived the monastery of Deir Mar Musa in Syria, which had been founded in the sixth century, adorned with beautiful frescoes in the eleventh century, and abandoned in the nineteenth century. The members of that monastery not only take the classical monastic vows of poverty, chastity, and obedience; they also commit themselves to work, contemplation, hospitality, and a love for Islam. This has enabled them to overcome the barriers of distrust and enmity that are as old as the Crusades. They consciously connect elements of their Christian faith with elements of Islam. This smacks of syncretism, of course; the community readily accepts this criticism. But Dall'Oglio and his community are convinced that, at a fundamental level, there is a faith that binds the faithful of the two religions together. Dall'Oglio has experienced that people who have grown up in religious traditions steeped in histories of confrontation need to dig even deeper to find the roots for

---

30. Küng, *Global Responsibility*, p. xv.

a just and peaceful relationship. Obviously, by going out of their accustomed ways to befriend their Muslim neighbors, the members of the Deir Mar Musa community hope to help overcome the infernal cycle of fear and violence that holds the Middle East in its grip. Dall'Oglio says: "People who do not go to their roots, but follow only the letter [of whatever sacred text], are the real troublemakers of this world. Follow them and we are doomed."[31]

This is but one example of the radical nature of faith ("radical" in its original Latin meaning: *radix* for "root"). It follows that those who claim to possess the meaning of their faith, be it Jewish, Christian, Muslim, or any other, are not radical enough. They have taken their faith into their own hands — and betrayed it. The apocalyptic scenarios that attract too many Christians and Muslims are no exception: they betray the *radix,* the root from which they both come, the God whose essence is love.

31. Robert B. Kaiser, "A Voice in the Wilderness," *Company* (online magazine of the Jesuits), April 27, 2004: www.companymagazine.org/v213/wilderness.htm. Further information about the monastery is at the website of the Monastery of Deir Mar Musa al-Habashi in Syria: www.deirmarmusa.org (accessed Jan. 21, 2006).

CHAPTER 8

Reinventing America

—◦◦◦—

In his first inaugural address, President Bill Clinton said that the time had come for "the vision and courage to reinvent America," adding that "each generation of Americans must define what it means to be an American." But in the same speech he assured his fellow citizens that "there is nothing wrong with America that cannot be cured by what is right with America."[1]

What about reinventing America? And what do I as a non-American have to do with it? One portion of the answer is that, though I am a German citizen, I am also in part American. Not by choice, but by the simple fact that the world I live in is largely shaped by the United States, the "American way of life," and the political, economic, and international policies designed and executed in Washington, D.C. Therefore, imagining what America can and should be concerns me as a foreigner as well. In other words, the future of America's "messianic project" has become a project that affects humanity as a whole. To many people around the world, it is a cause for hope; to many others, it is a reason for fear and suspicion.

1. Bill Clinton, "First Inaugural Address, January 21, 1993," The Avalon Project at Yale Law School: http://www.yale.edu/lawweb/avalon/presiden/inaug/clinton1.htm (accessed Jan. 20, 2006).

America at the Center: Three Approaches

"The international community, with America at its center, is history's unfinished masterpiece."[2] This is an amazing statement, made by a very prominent writer at *Newsweek,* one of the most widely read magazines in the world. I'm sure that quite a few people in the world today would say, "If this international community is history's 'masterpiece,' then history is a poor artisan!" Yet, masterpiece or not, there is a lot of truth in this sentence, which opens the concluding chapter, "Toward a New Consensus," of Michael Hirsh's book *At War with Ourselves* (2003). There he discusses the role of the United States with regard to the "rest of the world" at the beginning of the twenty-first century. According to his understanding, the situation is paradoxical in many ways: unprecedented might is mingled with unprecedented vulnerability. In spite of its overwhelming military power, the United States remains a part of the global network of peoples. In fact, it is at the center simply because it is the most important political, economic, and cultural factor in the world today. And in order to play this part most successfully, the United States must be interested in creating congenial conditions around the globe. In other words, it must intend to establish the same values and rights in all parts of the earth by which the United States is ruled itself. Hirsh quotes Henry Kissinger: "The dominant trend in American foreign-policy thinking must be to transform power into consensus so that the international order is based on agreement rather than reluctant acquiescence."[3]

Writing in 2003, Hirsh is obviously worried that the "überpower" of the United States is being used to create an empire that rules the world by brute force alone. But this would be a betrayal of the values and ideals that have made the United States the global power it is today. It would also be a betrayal of the great efforts the United States has made to establish the basic values and rules of the international community. Here Hirsh refers mainly to the United Nations and its

2. Michael Hirsh, *At War with Ourselves* (Oxford/New York: Oxford University Press, 2003), p. 237.

3. Hirsh, *At War with Ourselves,* p. 239.

suborganizations, such as the World Bank, the International Monetary Fund, the Bretton Woods institutions, but also, and not least, the International Criminal Court in the Hague. The United States must be committed to building and sustaining this international community because it is a system that provides a high degree of openness and democracy to the world's peoples. And "openness and democracy define who we are."[4]

Hirsh tries to reconcile the classic American insularity with the equally classic American universalism. He argues in favor of a "soft" hegemony, balanced by a resolute support of the structures that sustain international cooperation. Hence he wants the United States to contribute generously — in fact, much more generously than it has up to this point — to the establishment of just and peaceful global conditions. Yet, at the same time, the nation must maintain its military posture as a powerful global policing force. Hirsh continues:

> We *have* created, more powerfully than ever before, "an integrated international society"; there *do* exist, more deeply rooted than ever before, international institutions, international public opinion, and, yes, something like an international conscience. And in these unprecedented conditions lies the hope that the advantages of this integrated international community, secured by American power, are more tempting than the advantages of war, anarchy, and withdrawal from that system.[5]

It would be too easy, I think, to dismiss Hirsh's argument as a slightly "liberal" voice within the noisy chorus of the "neoconservatives" celebrating the "American empire."

The problems I have with Hirsh's book are on another level. He seems to assume that it is the decision of the United States alone whether and how it wants to be an active partner in the "international community." He does not take any time to consider the reasons for the widespread massive resentment among the world's peoples toward the United

4. Hirsh, *At War with Ourselves,* p. 256 (italics added).
5. Hirsh, *At War with Ourselves,* pp. 257f.

States. He gives the impression that America's long history of guilt and violence, along with other nations' counter-histories of humiliation and impotence written into this international community, can be easily discarded. In other words, his thinking about America's role in the world is still clouded by the myth of America's messianic innocence. The other aspect I find missing is the environmental issue. Hirsh shows no concern for the role of the United States in, and the impact of its way of life on, a world situation that is under the shadow of global warming, shrinking natural resources, and a growing world population.

The second approach I wish to investigate carries a decidedly different tone. Robert Bellah, the distinguished sociologist of civil religion who has diagnosed America's problems more succinctly than most,[6] says: "America is the center of a new kind of empire, but it is the only empire there is. Americans are, like it or not, citizens of that empire and responsible for the whole world."[7] Bellah goes on to say: "Our reaction to September 11 suggests that we are far from ready for that responsibility."[8] He gives the reason for that statement in the foreword to a book on American myths by Richard Hughes, and these two authors agree that it is the "myth of innocence" that renders the global power play of the United States so ominous:

> Neither our military nor our economic intervention in the rest
> of the world has been innocent. No empire with any duration
> has ever believed in its own innocence. Humility about who we
> are and what we can do is essential if we are to avoid the many
> disasters that await us.[9]

Here is a clear indication that great American thinkers such as Bellah and Hughes are aware that a profound reversal of America's leading myths is necessary in order to reinvent a fresh vision for the United

6. Esp. in Bellah, *The Broken Covenant: American Civil Religion in Time of Trial,* 2nd ed. (Chicago/London: University of Chicago Press, 1992).

7. Robert Bellah, in the foreword to Richard T. Hughes, *Myths America Lives By* (Urbana and Chicago: University of Illinois Press, 2003), p. xi.

8. Hughes, *Myths,* p. xi.

9. Hughes, *Myths,* p. xii.

States. Richard Hughes's book is an exercise in what I have been calling "deep remembering." As he discusses the American myths, he also gives space to those who have suffered from them. His focus is on the African-Americans (he could just as well have focused on Native Americans) to demonstrate that "our American myths have sometimes obscured and subverted the promise of the American Creed, especially for its minority populations."[10] By presenting their reactions, Hughes hopes to hint at the reservations that peoples around the globe have concerning American superpower.

Third, I want to refer to a statement by German theologian Jürgen Moltmann:

> As a self-governing people, America is what Franklin D. Roosevelt called the bold and lasting experiment of modern Western times. This democratic commonwealth is indeed, as Bill Clinton has said, a human invention. . . . The United States was consciously "founded" on the basis of the Declaration of Independence, the Constitution and the Bill of Rights. American civil rights are derived from human rights, and themselves point to the fact that "all men are created free and equal." In this respect the United States is a country — and the first country — for all humanity. Its claim and its promise is a body politic for humanity founded on human rights for each and all, which will surmount national states, and guarantee world peace.
>
> Consequently, the United States will remain historically unfinished and imperfect until this political experiment that humanity is making with itself succeeds or fails. American democracy remains incomplete as long as the whole world has not been won for democracy. That makes this experiment a messianic experiment. If it succeeds there will be an era of peace for all human beings; if it fails the world of human beings will perish in violence, injustice and war — and not the human world alone, but the world of nature, too.[11]

10. Hughes, *Myths*, p. 9.
11. Moltmann, *Coming of God*, p. 175.

Moltmann's thoughts reflect a fascination with the founding vision of the United States that has attracted millions of immigrants and informed the quest of groups throughout the world for the establishment of human rights. But Moltmann is also enough of a realist to see that the present state of the American experiment cannot be globalized to embrace all of humanity: "Politically, humanity cannot afford more than 'one America', and the same can be said ecologically of the earth. If the whole world were 'America', the whole world would already have been destroyed."[12] Moltmann adds that the idea of messianism itself is compromised by the historic millennialism that characterizes so much of the American dream. He says: "There is awareness of this ambiguity in America, inasmuch as 'the American nightmare' (Malcolm X) is following hard on the heels of the American dream, and American messianism is closely pursued by American apocalyptic."[13]

In their different ways, Hirsh, Bellah, and Moltmann are all wrestling with the paradox that characterizes the American experiment. Many people within the United States, plus many more around the world, are aware of the fact that its actual performance does not correspond adequately to the visions expressed in its foundational documents. In former centuries, people thought of America as the "New World," set apart from the "old" world by two oceans, a huge "haven of freedom" committed to a democratic experiment the world had never seen before. But now the United States is no longer that alternative world; it sits right in the middle of the "global village," now surrounded by others. This is what is implied in Hirsh's term "center," and it signifies an image shift that many citizens of the United States may well find uncomfortable.

The term "center" implies that there is a world around it, a periphery; and in their different ways, Hirsh, Bellah, and Moltmann express their grave worries about the ways in which the relationship between the center and the periphery is being shaped. The classic empire model is one in which the center *robs* the periphery of its resources. This is what Rome did — what made it rich and what caused its col-

12. Moltmann, *Coming of God*, p. 177.
13. Moltmann, *Coming of God*, p. 177.

lapse. And this is what the United States and the other highly industrialized nations of Europe and Asia are doing right now. Therefore, these three authors argue in favor of a model in which the center *shares* its resources with the periphery by extending its way of life to embrace the entire human family. This means, in Moltmann's words, that the American experiment must become the "political experiment that humanity is making with itself." The values and ideals proclaimed in the founding documents of the United States must become the values and ideals of all. In ideal terms, humanity becomes "America."

Moltmann says little about what this paradigm shift would cost. But he does indicate that the center-periphery image has to be broadened to include the ecological reality. The international community, with the United States as its central power, is itself surrounded by the natural community: the planet earth as its final — and finite — space. Even though this is so obvious an observation that it hardly needs mentioning, most people in the United States and Europe continue to deny this fact and go on living as if we had a second world sitting somewhere in a supply warehouse. We are so used to thinking that our world is endless and that its resources are inexhaustible that we cannot and will not comprehend the radical newness of our global predicament. Moltmann accentuates this dilemma by saying that the American experiment is incompatible with the carrying capacities of the earth. The *homo Americanus* is unfit, so it seems, to function within the limits of this finite home. (Again, I do not speak just of the citizens of the United States but of all those of us who share in the "American way of life" of comfortable consumption.)

It comes down to this question: What kind of ecological paradigm shift does *homo Americanus* have to make in order to create a planet that is environmentally sustainable? This sounds like a very technical matter; but it has a direct, and in many cases a diastrous, impact on the lives of our children and grandchildren. In his first inaugural address, Bill Clinton proclaimed that "America's long heroic journey must go forever upward."[14] If "forever upward" means unlimited progress toward ever more material riches and military powers, that is

14. Clinton, "First Inaugural."

dangerously naive. I fear that, fifty years from now, our grandchildren — if they are still alive — will curse the negligence and egotism in which we, both America itself and those in privileged countries who have developed its habits, have squandered their heritage.

Messianism and Vulnerability

"Reinventing America"? To speak of such an idea requires a massive paradigm shift. In quoting from Hirsh, Bellah, and Moltmann, I have attempted to show that our situation at the beginning of the twenty-first century is marked by a new level of global vulnerability. In the preceding chapter I summed up the four basic aspects of that vulnerability: (1) the constant threat of human self-annihilation by nuclear weapons and atomic energy production; (2) global climate change; (3) the increasing disparities between the rich and poor regions of the earth, intensified by wars over access to vital natural resources; (4) growing confrontations between state-controlled military powers and smallscale "terrorist" warfare with the ensuing consequences for human rights standards.

These global problems could be arranged in a different order. My point is simply that these, or similar, factors enable us to understand what *vulnerability means today*. It describes not only our existential reality, that is, the weakness of our bodies and the mortality of each individual life; it also describes our cosmic reality, the finiteness of the very systems of life on planet earth. Previous generations were used to accepting their individual vulnerability as inevitable, but they took comfort in the belief that life itself was invulnerable and would go on forever. The human beings of today, however, must come to terms with the unprecedented fact that all of life as we know it has come under the threat of widespread disaster, if not all-out extinction. This is the context that gives a pressing urgency to our reflections on America's messianic experiment.

Does this mean that this historical project is finished? I don't think so. Everything, of course, depends on how America adjusts to the cosmic vulnerability that has become humanity's overarching context. As

Richard Hughes has shown, there is a great deal in America's founding myths that remains valuable and can be developed further, provided America is prepared to include the truth of its victims. This is the approach of deep remembering: the process in which all partners, the winners and the losers, get the space to tell their stories. This will then lead to a fresh discourse about the nature of power and the reality of guilt. The myth of innocence is not necessarily linked to the myth of the chosen people. In fact, chosenness acquires its profundity only when it is capable of including failure and guilt — and thus the element of repentance. When it is understood in this way, power can be seen as empowering others rather than depriving others of their gifts for one's own benefit. Accordingly, the notion of "success" has a different face: it is oriented toward improving the community and makes the winner-loser syndrome obsolete. Success, then, is subservient to just and fair relationships between the members of communities. If "might makes right," the victims have nothing to hope for.

Change, repentance, empowerment, and justice belong to the context in which I would also put the notion of freedom. Freedom is the sovereignty with which a person, a group, or a nation conducts its affairs. Freedom comes from within and cannot be handed out as a gift.[15] In short, the context of global vulnerability helps the American nation redirect the notion of messianism. Not only does it help get rid of the messianic distortions we have seen in earlier parts of this book; more importantly, it establishes a fresh relationship between the well-being of the larger community, the "periphery," and the "mission" of its central agents. The recognition of living as gifted, albeit finite, beings within a blessed, though equally finite, global system can serve as the anchor of the messianic energies.

15. This explains in part why the name "Operation Iraqi Freedom" was chosen for the pre-emptive war against Iraq, and why it created so much resentment, most of all within Iraq. It was not, as we can see thus far, the freedom of Iraqis, by Iraqis, for Iraqis (to borrow Abraham Lincoln's famous formula), but rather the freedom of the U.S. to secure its interests in Iraq and the Middle East. Pressed for justification of the war after several pretexts have melted away, President Bush has often said that it was done to make the United States itself more secure.

Reconciliation Politics — an American Option?

In chapter 5, I began to talk about reconciliation politics, and I want to pursue this theme in an attempt to suggest a different face for America's messianic quest.[16] When I use the term "reconciliation politics," I intentionally combine the religious concept of reconciliation with the secular notion of politics. In the European context, many politicians and political advisers are reluctant to mix religion (as a supposedly private thing) with politics (as a public and necessarily pluralistic affair). They point negatively to Muslim efforts to subordinate democratic institutions to a theocratic order, as is the case in Iran and, more obliquely, in Saudi Arabia. They also consider the influence of conservative Protestant groups on political institutions in the United States to be far too great. On the other hand, the youth riots in many French cities during the fall of 2005 have shown that a radically secularized government such as France's does not know how to relate to those segments of the population with strong religious — in this case, Muslim — traditions. In some instances, Muslim organizations were the ones to mitigate the conflict.

Generally speaking, the public discourse that constitutes and sustains a democratic society should be interested in pursuing an intensive dialogue with people from the religious sector. What we need is more religious literacy, in other words, a conscious public debate about the goals, insights, and shortcomings of the various religious groups. I believe that that is the only way to integrate their possible contributions and to prevent the kinds of maneuvers where religious pressure groups hijack democratic parties or governments, or, with influence running

16. Reconciliation politics is being pursued at various levels and throughout the world. I wish to mention with special gratitude the peace-maker teams, mainly inspired by the historic peace churches, such as the Quakers and Mennonites. (As I write this, the Christian Peacemakers team remains missing in Iraq since November 2005.) The Eastern Mennonite University in Harrisonburg, VA, provides excellent researchers and training facilities. Two more international agencies with direct access to civil society groups engaged in reconciliation work merit special mention: the African Peacebuilding and Reconciliation Network, based in Nairobi, Kenya, under the leadership of Ethiopian scholar Hizkias Assefa; and the European Centre for Conflict Prevention, directed by Dutch researcher Paul van Tongeren, based in Utrecht, The Netherlands.

in the other direction, political parties co-opt certain religious groups as part of their grass-roots campaigns.

With these reservations in mind, I would like to suggest ways in which reconciliation politics can be a useful tool by which to approach deeply entrenched political divisions within and between nations.

1. Reconciliation politics strives to prevent provocative attitudes and confrontational behavior. Since it starts from a conviction that the other, including the enemy, is not essentially different from us, because we are all human beings, it will always look for the connecting elements, especially when the "other's" positions and attitudes differ radically from ours. This applies especially to dealing with fundamentalist groups, offensive and arrogant though their postures may be. That is why Rabbi Marc Gopin, peace researcher at George Mason University in Fairfax, Virginia, insists on meeting fundamentalists with deep respect.[17] Their sincerity and commitment must be honored, he feels, and one must be prepared to have one's own sincerity and commitment challenged. As a rule, reconciliation politics works from the assumption that there is an identity beyond the conflicting identities of groups, parties, and peoples. This is the identity of our shared humanity, which we experience in the vulnerability that is common to every one of us. This ultimate connectedness as members of the human family is the reference point of all human rights efforts. The fact that all human beings need the same inalienable rights implies that they are fundamentally capable of mutual discourse and reconciliation.

2. Reconciliation politics takes seriously the fact that guilt and shame are an inevitable part of how people deal with each other. Age-old histories of oppression and humiliation are intertwined in the lives of nations. They form the primordial soup that creates typical prejudicial conflict patterns. As new conflicts emerge, they tend to be organized according to the structure of conflicts that have long ceased to exist. A telling example is the frame of reference provided by the experience of "crusade." Although contemporary conflicts have nothing in

---

17. Marc Gopin, *Between Eden and Armageddon: The Future of World Religions, Violence and Peacemaking* (Oxford/New York: Oxford University Press, 2000), esp. pp. 199ff.

common with the medieval Crusades, they are still considered in the light of the old shameful experiences. The "winners" of history's battles are quick to forget the past; the "losers" decidedly are not. Thus there is the need to decontaminate past conflicts, to take the painful sting out of old wounds by means of deep remembering, a frank exchange about the things that are the lurking in the past, always waiting to jump into action in the midst of whatever conflicts arise.

These exchanges of deep remembering can be very difficult and often require considerable time and effort. One example is the tribunals for war criminals that began with the Nuremberg and Tokyo trials (following World War II); another is the tribunal convened in The Hague following the Balkan wars; a third is the most recent tribunal, which has been convened in Arusha in response to the genocide of the Tutsi people, mostly by Hutus. These efforts are extremely important, not least because they establish the sovereignty of law, which is perhaps the greatest civilizing achievement in the lives of human beings. Yet they do not succeed at extracting the poison from old wounds. As a rule, these tribunals are directed at the guilty parties and the punishment of their crimes; but they achieve little when it comes to lifting up the victims and restoring their dignity.

Therefore, an additional way is being developed to both search for the truth of past crimes *and* to facilitate reconciliation. This is the approach of the Truth and Reconciliation commissions, an instrument that has been used in over thirty cases to shed light on human rights violations and state terror.[18] What these efforts have in common is the emphasis on the fate of the victims and the suffering of their relatives; in most cases, a punishment of the perpetrators was either politically unfeasible or only partly achievable. Despite this limitation, further commissions are in preparation. They prove that there is a growing awareness among human beings around the world that unredeemed

18. See Priscilla B. Hayner, *Unspeakable Truth — Confronting State Terror and Atrocity* (New York/London: Routledge, 2001); see also United States Institute for Peace Library, "Truth Commission's Digital Collection," United States Institute of Peace: www.usip.org/library/truth.html (accessed Jan. 20, 2006). See also my evaluation of the South African Truth and Reconciliation Commission, in Müller-Fahrenholz, *The Art of Forgiveness,* pp. 85-101.

histories are dangerous time bombs. The explosive mixture of guilt and shame must be addressed so that people can be liberated from the evil that chains them to the past. There can be no freedom among or reconciliation between the peoples of today as long as they have not been set free from the bondage of past wounds.

Reconciliation politics, therefore, can be understood as a conscious effort to clean up the dangerous residues of past injustices and crimes. This is a task that should not be delegated to some interest groups or history departments, though those groups can help. This task must be conceived of as a vital component of internal and international relations. In other words, even though most politicians will shy away from it, it is a political task.

3. Once political partners agree to go through this process of deep remembering together, they will have to come to terms concerning the necessary elements of such a process. There is no way to avoid the necessity of an apology. The perpetrator side will have to agree to the elaboration of a comprehensive picture of the crimes committed. The truths that need to be told will have four aspects:

- the criminal activity must be clearly named and recognized;
- the story of this criminal activity must unfold as specifically as possible;
- the regret about the criminal activity must be expressed clearly;
- the readiness to offer compensations must be clear.[19]

One of the goals of the above process is to regain what could be called "moral sovereignty" with regard to past crimes and hurts. Both the honor of the victims and the self-respect of the perpetrators need to be restored so that they can meet each other face to face. Reconciliation politics, therefore, is not primarily about financial amends; there are many ways that compensations can be negotiated. The main

---

19. See Aaron Lazare, *On Apology* (London/New York: Oxford University Press, 2004). Lazare also speaks of four components in the reconciliation process: (1) acknowledgment of the offense; (2) communication of remorse and the related attitudes of forbearance, sincerity, and honesty; (3) explanation; (4) reparation.

aim is for the former enemies to create a new relationship built on mutual confidence.

4. It is not surprising that processes of reconciliation politics often stop at the first step, the matter of the apology. This is certainly a painful moment: the acknowledgment of guilt is always a bitter thing, and it is often "inadmissible" to people and political parties who are caught up in the winner-loser ideology. I need not discuss this question further, but my point is this: the admission of guilt is an indication of moral greatness and sovereignty that befits all peoples and nations. We need more "winners" who are sovereign enough to admit their misdeeds. Unfortunately, an apology, especially among political parties, is often equated with an admission of defeat and thus is seen as a cowardly act. Reconciliation politics, on the other hand, remains aware that the re-establishment of constructive relationships after a prolonged period of conflict, war, or human rights violations requires the will to negotiate compromises. These must be honorable compromises, to be sure, but agreements that include the renunciation of positions that formerly appeared to be non-negotiable. Obviously, such an approach is unacceptable to those with a superheroic cast of mind. It demands a different kind of heroism, one that sets the well-being of the wider community above one's own interests.

5. As we look at the challenges of the twenty-first century, reconciliation politics is nothing other than *Realpolitik*. Reconciliation may sound idealistic, or even romantic, but it flows from a realistic assessment of the global human situation. And this requires an understanding that reconciliation politics has an ecological dimension. As I have said before, the global vulnerability that marks our time forces all of humanity to seek ways of getting along with each other as profitably, fairly, and justly as possible. And this work needs to be placed within the environmental perspective, because it is planet earth that sets the limits for everything we earthlings are doing (all the escapist *Star Trek* fantasies about settling on other planets notwithstanding). Thus, the overriding focus for all peoples on earth must be to keep this earth inhabitable. How can the needs of human beings be reconciled with the functioning integrity of the ecosphere in which we exist?

This question needs to be addressed primarily by those nations that find themselves at the "center" simply because they make up the heaviest burden for Mother Earth. Therefore, exemplary efforts of conversion must be expected from them. It would be unrealistic, of course, to assume that the grave economic, cultural, and social disparities between the world's peoples can be leveled out completely. And we can expect that new occasions for violent conflicts will emerge. Nonetheless, the goal must be to settle for systems of sustainable neighborhoods that manage to stay within the carrying capacities of our global homeland. It follows, then, that we "earthlings" need to develop an *earth patriotism* that takes priority over our national patriotisms. Systems of sustainable neighborhoods need to enjoy a certain amount of security. The main institution to safeguard the required legal and social standards must be the United Nations, with the United States offering its overwhelming powers to this task.

6. There is much that religious institutions and humanitarian movements can do to promote the goals and methods of reconciliation politics. The importance of the international scientific community can hardly be underestimated. Global scientists have to play significant roles in engaging people from all over the world and helping them move beyond accustomed barriers of race, gender, caste, and religion. Non-governmental organizations (NGOs) are the ones to facilitate dialogues, prepare apologies, and develop possible compensatory strategies.[20] Most of all, they can inspire trust where government officials have sown hatred. They are the ones who may be able to produce good will and honest beginnings in opposition to all who thrive on exploitation and corruption.

The Counsel of the Prophet Micah

I have found it difficult to sketch out these aspects of reconciliation politics, mainly because a voice inside tells me that it's not worth it,

20. For a good example of the wealth of programs that can be promoted by the international networks of civil society actors, see Paul van Tongeren, Malion Brenk, Marte Hellema, Juliette Verhoeven, eds., *People Building Peace II: Successful Stories of Civil Society* (Boulder/London: Lynne Rienner Publishers, 2005).

that it's already too late, that those in control will laugh me off the stage. Though I tell myself — given the global realities — that reconciliation politics makes more sense than the retaliation politics we are witnessing every day, the political status quo keeps telling me that today's leading powers read the global realities in opposite ways. Particularly, it seems, the current leadership of the United States, the central power of world affairs, is determined to pursue a decidedly different agenda.[21]

So where are we headed? I do not believe that there will be a conversion to reconciliation politics under the present U.S. administration. I do not believe that any acknowledgment of America's historical guilt can be expected in the near future. And the temptation of America's quasi-divine omnipotence is too great to consider a revision of its mythical sense of exceptionality. There will probably be no attempts to convert essential parts of the military-industrial complex to serve civilian and humanitarian means anytime soon. And regarding the political leadership in Europe, no nation that is prominent enough appears to be courageous enough to develop an alternative vision. The alternative *must* come from within the superpower, and I am certain that it will.

Sooner or later — and the sooner the better — a president of the United States, perhaps even along with a contingent of prominent members of Congress, will have to say, "We are sorry." This would be the sovereignty in accordance with America's power and a proof of its greatness. This would set the stage for other nations to enter comparable processes; for the world is full of age-old crimes that are waiting to be redeemed through reconciliation.

Way back in 1630, aboard the *Arbella*, the Honorable John Winthrop preached a sermon entitled "A Modell of Christian Charity." In this pivotal text, where Winthrop lays out the articles of charity as the elements required by the covenant with God, he speaks of the blessings

---

21. I get comfort from the most unexpected places. Thomas Friedman is arguing more and more fervently in favor of a major paradigm shift, away from an economy based on oil toward an economy focusing on regenerative energy supplies. See Thomas L. Friedman, "New 'Sputnik' Challenges: They All Run on Oil," *New York Times*, Jan. 20, 2006, p. A17.

to be expected if the people obey the covenant; but he is also very clear about the punishments to be feared if the people turn away from it.[22]

But how are the people to avoid the "shipwreacke" to which he refers? He invokes the "counsell of Micah, to do justly, to love mercy, to walk humbly with our God" (Micah 6:8). One of the most eminent among the Founding Fathers of the United States, Winthrop knew that the "counsell of Micah" is one of those "fundamentals" always to be remembered by peoples and their governments. It speaks of the three primordial criteria for just power — justice, mercy, and humility. These three criteria guide the use of power, and they contain its abuse.

Perhaps the most difficult virtue to put into practice is humility, especially for the people of the United States. Have not their leaders told them again and again that they are the greatest? Have they not been made to believe that the level of their superpower borders on omnipotence and that they have nothing to fear? It would appear, then, that humility is irreconcilable with America's global mission; indeed, it smacks of weakness and cowardice. But the opposite is true. The word "humility" is related to the Latin word *humus,* meaning "earth." Humility is the virtue that keeps us close to the earth; it keeps us truthful to our human condition and one with all living creatures that share this earth with us. Humility, therefore, is of paramount importance, especially for those who are entrusted with great power. Humility is the antidote to the disorder inherent in what the Greeks called *hubris,* the arrogance of power that is bound to be the beginning of the end.

22. John Winthrop, "A Modell of Christian Charity," posted by Hanover College: http://history.hanover.edu/texts/winthmod.html (accessed Jan. 29, 2006).